Social Psychological Theories:

A Comparative Handbook for Students

Social Psychological Theories:

A Comparative Handbook for Students

Carl J. Slawski

California State University, Long Beach

Scott, Foresman and Company   Glenview, Illinois

Dallas, Tex.   Oakland, N.J.   Palo Alto, Cal.   Tucker, Ga.   London

Cover photograph by George Obremski

Library of Congress Cataloging in Publication Data

Slawski, Carl J 1938-
  Social psychological theories.

  Bibliography: p. 181
  Includes index.
  1. Social psychology. I. Title.
HM251.S6255   320   80-21201
ISBN 0-673-15333-9

1 2 3 4 5 6—RRC—85 84 83 82 81 80

This book is dedicated to the visionary
builders of better societies and better
relationships founded on their
collectively strong sense of self and
community—to the searchers
after both self-actualization and
SOCIAL ACTUALIZATION

Preface

Social Psychological Theories is a handbook and compendium of virtually all the major and distinct contemporary perspectives in social psychology. Each of the sixteen perspectives is boiled down to a minimum of technical jargon and presented in a way that will be easily applicable to the life of the beginning student in social science. Because research data are of interest mainly to the professional or advanced major in the field of psychology or sociology, that content is left for the recommended readings listed in the Appendix. An average of two readings per chapter are introduced in the Appendix, followed by study questions for discussion. The introductory chapter defines the key elements of the approach of the handbook and sets the stage from the point of view of the philosophy of social science and formal theory construction.

The handbook is aimed at students taking their first course in social psychology in either a sociology or psychology department. It should prove quite useful for review by students in related courses, such as small groups, marriage and the family, or contemporary sociological theory. Graduate students should find it particularly useful for reviewing the subject matter for comprehensive examinations or cognate seminars.

My purpose in writing *Social Psychological Theories* was to reformulate the essential concepts and hypotheses of social psychology in hopes of some future synthesis, as well as to put it all in language and a format both understandable and immediately applicable to the lives of students. I have tried to include coverage of more perspectives than is typical, and to use simpler, more accessible language. Furthermore, this text is set up for application to numerous real-life situations, plus drama, films, biographies, and simulations.

In long-range preparation of this book I am grateful for the legacy betokened by the opportunity to work with, and the seminars and courses I took as a student from, such persons as Norman Denzin, Herbert Blumer, Tamotsu Shibutani, Milt Bloombaum, Tom Scheff, Irving Lazar, Ed Hulett, Gene Summers, Harold Garfinkel, Harold Kelley, David Epperson, Walter Buckley, and W. Ross Ashby. In preparation of the manuscript I appreciate the kindness of Walter Dinteman and the patient copyediting of Doris Donald. Thanks are due as well to Allen Johnson for the use of his life story, originally written up for my class in social psychology; to Edna Elizabeth McCutchen for use of the excerpt from her paper; and to the hundreds of students in my classes who taught me how to teach them social psychology.

Carl J. Slawski
Long Beach, California

Notes from the Author

Social Psychological Theories deals with a very wide range of theories in social psychology. It includes a brief sampling of all the major and distinct contemporary perspectives that have been closely linked with the traditions of the discipline. Today, the discipline of social psychology is concentrating on laboratory-bound small-scale and middle-range hypothesis testing. Though this small-scale conceptualizing is sophisticated and valuable, the separate perspectives of social psychology need to be raised to the scale of a full-blown theory, that is, to be tied together in a set of deductively interrelated hypotheses backed by empirical evidence. This text engages in such theory building.

The field of social psychology also needs an introductory text that facilitates application of basic social psychological principles to students' lives. Undergraduates often expect a course in social psychology to provide practical insights and explanations for everyday happenings and problems. Too often, they find themselves working in the laboratory or studying survey data analysis prepared by professional sociologists or psychologists. This is not to deny the importance of methodology and abstract principles to the scholarly discipline and to the professional researcher. Most students, however, especially nonmajors, are more interested in substance and theory rather than in laboratory research. This text brings together sixteen of the most important partial theories in social psychology and arranges them into five clusters, representing both the psychological and sociological points of view, and provides application of these theories to problems of everyday life.

The introductory chapter defines some philosophical and technical terms, and presents the general approach to comparing theories. It also defines the four modes of theory building, together with other crucial dimensions with which the various perspectives can be systematically and comparatively evaluated.

The introductions and critiques of each of the five parts help students locate theories in relation to one another. Each of the theories, readings, and introductions can also stand by itself. Each chapter begins with a summary of the perspective. The critiques after each of the five parts include sections on evaluation and application, which rate the theories on the basis of the four criteria necessary for a good theory. The critiques also include information and examples on how each theory can be employed to change a person and how to achieve self-actualization. Summaries are kept to the briefest essentials in order to facilitate theoretical comparison uninterrupted by confusing conceptual details and nuances. Furthermore, most of the readings are so basic that detailed descriptive introductions would be largely redundant. The theories can best be explained by applying them to ones' own experiences. Assignments that allow students to combine theory with their own experiences are included—the "Three-Page Everyday Applications," plus the "Comparative Write-Ups." These exercises can help students make the theories a natural part of their conceptual artillery when looking at the real, personal, and social world around them.

Two theories at a time are applied after each part—for a total of six theories applied to one story. Each application is followed by a comparative evaluation of the applied theories using the four criteria for a good theory. An additional excellent device for application is contained in the Appendix in the instructions for student preparation of classroom simulation games. Other pedagogical devices include study questions for each of the sixteen theories, found in the Appendix, as well as the "50-Word Summaries" of each theory (described after Part I), which are extremely useful for student understanding and review.

The readings suggested in the Appendix emphasize applications to everyday life, without neglecting empirical research. They include classic and basic studies as well as the newest schools of thought. The content of the recommended readings is broadly inclusive, ranging across such topics and problems as choosing a friend or a mate, mental illness, marital adjustment, small groups, changing people, and self-actualization. The data collection settings for the research articles represent all types—laboratory, survey, and participant observation. This coverage is brought out in the alternate table of contents, which can be used by student and teacher alike to more systematically compare methods and topics.

The concluding chapter briefly classifies the perspectives by disciplinary domain and approach to research. Then an attempt is made to sketch out a metatheoretical synthesis using the general systems theory. The overall goal of the book is to point the professional social psychologist toward a deductive, broad ranging, and synthetic theory—a theory or metatheory yet to be discovered. At the same time, the student should be stimulated in relevant ways to work toward a personal synthesis.

Skeptics will see this handbook as useful only for the advanced or bright student. My experience over the years is that it appeals to the interested and serious student, regardless of intelligence or GPA. In conclusion, I would like to stress the futility of skimming this volume as a guidebook, and the probable boredom of trying to read it like a monograph, or ordinary textbook. The ideas need to be put to use in analyzing life. It is certainly not a standard text. While it is based on largely academic theories, the original theorists themselves are not likely to recognize their own theories. The brevity of presentation and sketchy evaluations were arrived at after semesters of trial and continuing struggle to show how these theories can be made relevant to the present needs of most students. This is not intended to be a completely self-contained text. It is intended only to facilitate the learner's discovery of himself or herself in human groups and, in the process, to gather a few elementary notions about comparing *Social Psychological Theories*.

Contents

Introduction: Evaluating Theories   1

Part I   Humanistic-Developmental Theories   18

    Chapter 1:   Social Actualization   20

    **Chapter 2:   Identity Development
(Neo-Freudian Socialization)**   23

    Critique of Humanistic-Developmental Theories   26
    Review and Comparison   26
      Evaluation and Application   27
    Student Use Instructions: 50-Word Summary   30
    Everyday Application: Three-Page Write-Up   31
    Sample Student Write-Up   33

Part II   Structure and Change Theories   39

    Chapter 3:   Group Dynamics   41

    Chapter 4:   Role Bargaining   43
    Chapter 5:   Interparty Conflict   46

    Critique of Structure and Change Theories   49
    Review and Comparison   49
      Evaluation and Application   50
    Sample Comparative Write-Up   55

Part III Behavioristic Theories 60

Chapter 6: Stimulus-Response Behaviorism 62

Chapter 7: Exchange Theory 65

Chapter 8: Game Theory 66

Critique of Behavioristic Theories 69
Review and Comparison 69
Evaluation and Application 70

Part IV Congruency Theories 77

Chapter 9: Cognitive Dissonance 79

Chapter 10: Symmetry 81

Chapter 11: Interpersonal Congruence 83

Chapter 12: Self-Consistency 86

Critique of Congruency Theories 88
Review and Comparison 88
Evaluation and Application 89
Sample Comparative Write-Up 96
Everyday Application: Three-Page Write-Up 99

Part V Social Interaction Theories 100

Chapter 13: Symbolic Interactionism 103

Chapter 14: Labeling 105

Chapter 15: Dramaturgy   **109**

Chapter 16: Ethnomethodology   **111**

Critique of Social Interaction Theories   **115**
Review and Comparison   115
Evaluation and Application   117
Sample Comparative Write-Up   122

Conclusion: A Synthesis of Social Psychological Theories   127

Appendix

A. Format Sheets   140
B. Recommended Reading and Study
   Questions   143
C. Classroom Simulation Games   171
D. Comparative Rating of the Sixteen
   Perspectives   175
E. Journal Guidelines and Format   176

References   179

Bibliography   181

Alternate Table of Contents   183

Index   186

Social Psychological Theories:

A Comparative Handbook for Students

Introduction

Evaluating Theories[1]

Distinction will be made in this chapter in turn between a concept, a hypothesis, a theory, and a perspective; then of the relation between theory and data, the meaning of an operational definition, the four modes of theory construction, the nature of a theoretical problem as opposed to a social problem, and the need to comparatively examine each theory in light of its ability to explain change over time (t_1 to t_2) in a person or a group. The meaning of the four criteria for a good theory will be described along with a rationale for the approach taken in this text. These definitions, once understood in practice, will provide the student with a technique for analyzing any new theory he encounters. Their unfamiliarity, however, will mean that most students will not be very comfortable with them until they have done the applications to be suggested in the Critique and Application sections after each of the five parts of the text. Their presentation in the introductory chapter is necessary for pedagogical reasons, as well as for encouraging the student to reread this chapter on more than one occasion as the course progresses.

The term "theory" will most often be used in this book in a rather strict sense of the word. Most beginners, and not a few professional social scientists use "theory" in a very loose sense of the word. They implicitly define theory as a set of statements making use of abstract

---

[1]It is quite likely that many students in the average undergraduate course in introductory social psychology will not be able to assimilate all of the concepts in this chapter on first reading. This should be no obstacle, however, since the ideas will come up again and again, and should where necessary be supplemented by occasional review and classroom discussion. In order to avoid becoming bogged down in the philosophy of social science, some readers may want to skip this chapter and begin their reading with Chapter 1.

concepts to describe concrete events. By extension, their loose definition of **social theory** is the use of abstract concepts to describe some aspects of social structure or social change. Upon reflection, not to mention reference to the philosophy of social science, we can easily see that *concepts alone* do not explain the existence or *cause* of a certain social structure. Only a set of *hypotheses* can explain *why* anything happens. (On these points see, for example, H. Zetterberg, *On Theory and Verification in Sociology*, and G. Homans, *The Nature of Social Science*.) One concept at a time cannot explain a pattern of formal and informal communication among co-workers. Even a classificatory scheme or diagram of the relation between various concepts cannot in itself explain anything. A concept is simply an abstraction which focuses our attention on a certain regularity or recurrence of some phenomenon. It can thus, at best, only give information or help to *describe* what happens. A concept or classification of concepts cannot in itself explain why the social structure took its present form. Nor can concepts alone explain change in the structure of relations between people. And that is crucial. Again, only hypotheses begin to explain.

Let us clarify these notions with an example. The concept of alienation directs our attention to a discrepancy between the rules of interaction in a society or group, and to the feelings of behavior of particular members. Those members whose behavior disagrees with the rules or who feel powerless or out of step are said to be alienated. The concept itself merely focuses our attention on the phenomenon. It may help to describe the condition or state of the relationship between the alienated person and his group or society. But the concept alone does not explain how that person became alienated, nor how his condition or state of being alienated affects his relationship with fellow members of his society or group. For this reason, we say that a concept in itself has descriptive capability, or *information value* alone. Even a classification of types of alienation (such as powerlessness, meaninglessness, normlessness, or self-estrangement) still only focuses our attention on a particular kind of information about the concrete phenomenon.

Next we shall further explore the nature of a **hypothesis** and its relation to theory. We must put *two* or *more* separate *concepts* together in a statement that tells us something about the *causal* relationship between the two concepts. Then and only then can we begin to say *why* something happened. Then we may be able to partially *explain* something. In the language of social science we call such a statement about the relationship between concepts a hypothesis. Then when we put hypotheses together in logical order we have a theory, or at least a part of one. Nearly everyone agrees that an *explanation is a theory*, and a theory is an explanation. Hence, we can see that the basic building block of a theory is the hypothesis. Depending on the complexity of the phenomena we are trying to explain, we may need several hypotheses for a reasonably complete theory. The nature of the concrete and theoretical problem we are addressing will determine how systematic, precise, logical, and comprehensive our set of hypotheses must be.

To extend our example, we may state a hypothesis: *If* citizens have a high degree of alienation from their country, *then* the country will have a high suicide rate. Notice the formal presentation using the words "If . . . then . . . " to indicate before and after, or cause and effect, or antecedent and consequent. Such formal statement is not always necessary, but is frequently useful. At any rate, here we have a basically causal statement that is at least a tentative explanation or reason why there is a high suicide rate. While such statements at first blush may seem obvious, they are nonetheless necessary. Much of social science consists of seemingly obvious statements which must be made fully explicit to avoid ambiguity. If we do not do this, we will very likely fall prey to our stereotypes, preconceptions, or contradictory beliefs. If we do not state our explanations explicitly we cannot verify them. Nor can other researchers or observers check up on their reliability. *Reliability* is simply repeatability of observation of the same phenomenon from one observer or situation to the next. The *validity* of our observations will also be in doubt if we do not make our hypotheses explicit. Validity is concerned with whether we are actually observing the phenomenon we say we are observing. If the definitions of the concepts in our hypothesis are not clear as well as reliable and valid we are in trouble as scientists. We might then make better litterateurs. Shakespeare, as a litterateur, may be allowed the leisure of contradictory statements, but scientists must try to specify more precisely why such contradictory observations or phenomena occur in different circumstances. Such precision is not always exciting for the beginner in social science. Nevertheless, he must at least appreciate the need for precision before he can claim an understanding of even one branch of social science.

In the specific points of accuracy and completeness of theory we can see the weakness of virtually all social scientific theory. For this reason, we must now distinguish between a perspective and a theory. A **perspective** is merely a set of concepts, a partial or sub-theory used as a frame of reference or classificatory scheme for observation. It may be a partial, incomplete set of hypotheses which are not yet integrated in a fully logical way. We can now see that even though a well-formulated hypothesis may provide a part of an explanation, a *single* hypothesis is never more than merely a *part* of a theory. Strictly speaking, a **theory** is a set of deductively interrelated hypotheses. Although there have been some attempts to achieve it, there exists no relatively complete theory of the conditions and effects of alienation. This is par for the course of social science. This is the reason why in this text we frequently use the term *perspective* instead of *theory*. We have indeed brought together here sixteen separable perspectives, none of which can stand by itself as a theory in the strict sense. This should also be a constant reminder of the present incomplete state of theory in social psychology.

This fact of incompleteness should also help explain why there is no single theory of social psychology. This is why we will present no less than sixteen perspectives in five groups. Even the five groups as a whole cannot honestly be called separate theories. The relations of the separate perspectives within each group are still a long way from comprehensive, logically integrated statements. It should also be clear by now that our definition of a theory provides an ideal to work for as well as a starting point for analysis. Hardly any theorist today claims anything like completeness or a definitive statement of his theory or perspective. Yet there seems to be nothing like a program of serious communication between adherents of one set of perspectives with those of another. This is a serious fault reflecting not only our lack of knowledge in the relatively early years of social psychology as a discipline, but it also indicates the fragmentary nature of the vast majority of research, the lack of sound theory as a basis for research, as well as the individualism of those who call themselves social psychologists. Hopefully, the next generation will produce such a program of research and inquiry aimed at more sophistication as well as integration of theory. Maybe some students who read this text will be motivated in this direction. This is one of the author's long-range aims. However, until further developments occur along these lines it seems more fruitful to try to use two or three perspectives at once to systematically investigate the same single theoretical and social problem. This strategy is not only provocative for the professional social scientist, but can be fun for the student. After trying to explain a given phenomenon with two "theories," it is satisfying to evaluate the *relative utility* of each. For example, the student might try to evaluate the relative utility of actualization theory (Chapter 1) and cognitive dissonance (Chapter 9) for explaining the relation of alienation to the suicide rate.

THEORY VS. DATA

The relation of theory to research or data collection must also be clearly understood. There is no way to separate theory from methods in practice. Hence comes the following discussion of their interplay.

We have noted the importance of concepts in forming hypotheses, as well as the need for reliable and valid observations of the concepts of each hypothesis. It is absolutely essential for any research project that data be gathered not merely to illustrate but rather to provide some kind of test of the hypothesis being studied. For scientific purposes, these data or phenomena as observed must provide information about the separate concepts of the hypothesis in such a way that the causal relation between concepts can be proven or disproven. Due to the complexity of social reality, or of most hypotheses about people in groups, it is hardly possible to achieve definitive data in a single study for even the concepts of a single hypothesis. In this fact we have another reason for the lack of more synthetic theory in the discipline.

Data is preferably gathered and analyzed based on **operational definitions**. This is a definition of a concept in the form of a cook-book recipe for observing the occurrence of that concept in real social situations in a quantitative way. The result of such observations of the concept of alienation among assembly line workers in two automobile plants, for example, might yield an average rating among ten observers of high alienation in one plant, and medium alienation in the other. Operational definitions are almost always stated in a way that will produce quantitative results as far as possible. This may mean a rating from "1" to "10," or "high" to "low." An exception would be a case where the phenomenon observed either exists or does not, such as whether a person is married or not. Operational definitions are used in virtually all research that is called scientific, as an aid to objectifying the data. Humanistically oriented students of society, including humanistic psychologists, are more willing than laboratory or survey researchers to compromise with qualitatively deep and meaningful topics, such as the emotions of love, hate, joy, sorrow, and states of peak experience, self-actualization, or personal fulfillment. Such concepts can be quantified only with difficulty or not at all; hence, we must rely more heavily on case studies, interviews, personal documents, and participant observation in order to study such softer but more meaningful topics.

There are, in fact, many ways to approach the research enterprise. Sometimes these ways are called **modes of theory construction.** There are four basic modes (as summarized nicely by Melvin Marx, 1963), namely, 1) inductive, 2) deductive, 3) the model, and 4) the functional mode. These modes refer to the extent to which formalized inferences are explicitly used as guides to research. They are represented in Figure 1.1.

1) The **inductive mode** of theorizing results in hypotheses about empirical (data-based) relationships between concepts. This is the basis for the so-called "positivistic" view. Panel a, Figure 1.1,

FIGURE 1.1

Modes of Theory Construction

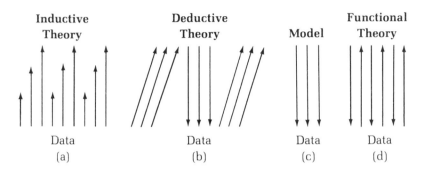

represents this view. The successively longer arrows indicate the progressive nature of the development of theory. The emphasis of researchers of this type is primarily on data collection. They basically assume that the theory will eventually take care of itself.

Any of the basic methods of data collection can be used for the inductive mode of theorizing. They include laboratory observation (such as the small groups lab); the social survey (interview or questionnaire); or participant observation (in which the researcher joins in the ongoing activities of the group being studied. The *case study* method is more comprehensive, and more or less independent of the method of data collection. More often it uses a combination of methods, including secondary analysis of personal and historical documents, along with direct participation and observation of the social group being studied. See the tabular alternative table of contents (p. 184) for reference to readings in this text which exemplify each mode of research or data collection.

2) The **deductive mode** of theory construction begins research with a theory or a set of explicit, formally interrelated hypotheses stated as carefully and logically as possible. Data collection and empirical research are closely based on the theory. In Panel b of Figure 1.1, the deductive mode is illustrated. The slanted arrows at the left indicate the relatively more overt development of the theory from empirical data. The slanted arrows at the right indicate the theorist's attempt to use data based on his theory to revise and improve the theory.

Ideally, every theory should be stated deductively, either at the beginning or at the end of a research project. This is the most clearly logical way to state a theory. And without such logical statement, a theory cannot readily be criticized or reviewed. But a *mode of statement* is not equivalent to a *mode of theory construction* or research per se. Nor is it to say that the deductive mode of theory building is necessarily the best. We are only saying that the deductive form of logical statement is usually most useful as a guide for later theorizing and research.

3) The **model** is an analogy used as a guide to research. For example, the physical model of the interrelationship of parts of the human body has been used to help describe the elements of society. The head could be the government, the hands the workers, the heart the family, etc. Or, the mathematical model of the computer and its program (with feedback loops) has been used to describe the process of communication between a person and his societal environment, or the mechanisms of the human brain. Obviously, some such analogies are better than others. But it should be noted that the model is quite exclusively a deductive mode of theorizing because it begins with theory and later tests the theory. It differs, though, from the previously treated deductive mode in the following ways. It is not directly based on data, nor does the theorist normally go very far in the direction of revising and improving this theory based on data collection. Rather, the data, if any, is more often used primarily to illustrate the model itself. This model mode is represented in Panel c of Figure 1.1. In general, the model is used to generate hypotheses, or to fit and piece together hypotheses already stated. If these hypotheses do not fit the model, either the hypotheses or the model must be discarded. There is relatively little interplay between theory and data here, especially compared to the inductive and functional modes.

4) The **functional mode** begins either with bits of data or with a small-scale or "middle-range" theory. It continually revises and improves the theory based on continuous data collection. It recognizes the imperfection of models and the lack of a truly empirically based "grand scale," or all-encompassing theory in contemporary social science. It is simultaneously inductive and deductive at once, in an ongoing program of research. Panel d of Figure 1.1 indicates the continual two-way traffic or interaction between data and theorizing. Neither the empirical nor the conceptual is more important than the other in the functional mode. Perhaps a more descriptive term for the functional mode would be the **reciprocating mode** of theory construction.

The reader should beware of confusing this functional mode of theory building (the term may be that of Melvin Marx) with the school of thought known as functional theory, or with the mere statement of functional hypotheses per se. There exist many textbooks in the history and construction of sociological and psychological theories and systems which explain this in detail. In general, functional theory deals with changes within a given social structure which have important consequences for the structure of society as a whole. Finally, functional hypotheses usually mean hypotheses in which one concept is a function of, or depends on, or varies with the other concept. Again, please do not confuse functional hypotheses or functional theory with what we here call the functional mode of theory construction.

THE THEORETICAL PROBLEM

In the author's experience, most beginning students of social science make the mistake of doing a paper on a *topic* rather than on a theoretical *problem*. The result is often a compilation of quotations or summaries of data with little theoretical relevance. We previously defined theory as a set of deductively interrelated hypotheses. From this we can infer that a social scientific or *theoretical problem*, as such, is a statement or hypothesis about social reality whose clarification or solution will be a genuine contribution to our knowledge about that reality. Every social scientific hypothesis or piece of research should ideally be based on or somehow be explicitly related to such a theoretical problem.

A theoretical problem may also be a *social problem*. But a social problem is not necessarily a theoretical problem until it is stated in a theoretical way. Alienation is a social problem since it implies negative consequences for members of a group or society which suffers from it. It is a weakness, imperfection, or conflict within a society that is recognized as such by the general public. In order to give this social problem theoretical relevance, we must first state it as a hypothesis, or somehow suggest how it is related to at least one other important theoretical concept. The following hypothesis strikes a happy balance, because it is at once a social as well as a theoretical problem: *When a sense of meaninglessness (a type of alienation) is felt by a high percentage of members of a society, then there will be a high rate of mental illness in that society.* The two basic concepts are the *sense of meaninglessness* and the *rate of mental illness*. Note that these concepts are stated in a way that would allow us to quantify each. The relation between the two is clearly stated. As meaninglessness goes up, so will the rate of mental illness. Thus, we have a social as well as a theoretical problem contained within one hypothesis. It is an ideal of research that answers to a theoretical problem will also shed light on some social problem. Even so-called "pure" research rather than applied research should do this, if possible.

We can go one step further in our attempt to integrate many

theories or perspectives, such as the sixteen treated in this volume. We can ask what is the single basic theoretical problem of all social science, for all theory and research. This is an attempt to develop a **metatheoretical** approach, or a theory about theories. The final chapter of this handbook will try to integrate the other theories by the use of the metatheory known as the **general systems** theory. Some philosophers saw the most basic problem as being how social order is possible. Hobbes asked why men do not end up in a war of all against all. Others attempt to explain the structure and functioning of social personalities, groups, and societies. It seems to this author that in order to adequately explain the structure of a social order, the theorist must explain how one kind of structure in that society *changed* into another at a later point in time, after the occurrence of some crucial *intervening event*. There may be many such precipitating events, and many points in time, but we can most simply formulate this notion by considering Figure 2.1. There we have represented a structure of a person, group or society at two points in time. The structure at time 1 is represented by square S_1. The structure of the same phenomenon which we are analyzing is represented at time 2 by square S_2. S_1 comes before, and S_2 after the crucial intervening (or precipitating) event ($= E$) which we conceive of as touching off or immediately causing the change in structure of that person, group, or society. The arrow (P) between the two structures represents the *process* by which that structure moves from its form at S_1 to its form at the later point in time, S_2. In short, the message here is that for a *theory to be complete, it must describe and explain all the elements of this diagram*, namely, the structure at two or more points in time (S_1 and S_2), the nature of the intervening event (E), and the process (P) by which the structure changed. If all this can be accomplished by a theory, and it is a big

FIGURE 2.1

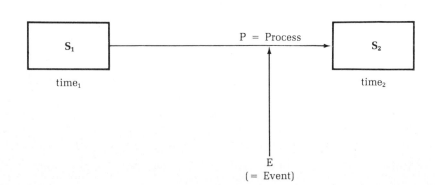

order, then we have explained social order, as well as social conflict, its causes, and resultant change. Surely no social theorist could ask for more.

Many other fascinating notions could be stated about the relations between this general theoretical problem and hypotheses and other individual theories. But for now that will be left to the evaluations of each theory after it is treated in the text. The student and teacher are encouraged to use their playful theoretical imaginations. This is in the last analysis the only hope for long run-theoretical breakthroughs. Ultimately, the attempt to apply the requisites for a general theoretical problem to each theory will be a highly thought-provoking exercise. A description of how to do this is contained in the instructions for student write-ups after Part II of this volume, followed by an illustration through the analysis of a theater play.

The goal of such student exercises as well as of this handbook as a whole is not reductionism, but rather an attempt to promote a synthesis and more general theory. Reductionism attempts to reduce explanations to concepts at a single level of abstraction. For example, a reductionist might try to reduce psychology to biology, or sociology to psychology. While a kind of limited reduction (or dealing with a limited number of concepts in a given analysis) is necessary to get a handle on complex problems, any attempt to reduce all social science to a monocausal theory is destined to failure. The history of social science is full of such attempts.

CRITERIA FOR EVALUATING A THEORY

With the preceding overview of the nature of social scientific theory, theoretical problems, and the modes of theory construction, the student has the seeds of what to look for when approaching a new social theory or problem. Innumerable other considerations could be discussed which, for certain limited, say classificatory purposes, might shed some light on the philosophy, substance, or methodology of social science. The number of possibilities is so great that many theorists and philosophers have alternatively written books and been baffled by the problem of evaluating theories comparatively. Classification, however, is not enough. Nor is it sufficient to analyze one theory at a time. Because of the complexity and abstractness of theories and evaluative criteria, we need a point-by-point comparison of two or more theories at a time. This approach is not only theoretically sound, not to mention neglected, but also pedagogically crucial. It is quite clear in addition that to compare two complex theories *as a whole* is a task suitable only for genius. Thus, our approach will be to suggest comparison of the main points of two or three theories at a time, as applied to a single instance of personal or social change over time. This strategy is also contained in the instructions for student write-ups after Part I.

Our task has been to reduce the huge number of possible evaluative criteria to the most important ones, without leaving out anything really essential to the nature of theory. On these grounds, four criteria seem necessary (cf. Slawski: 1974). In a natural chronological order of use for evaluating theory, they are: 1) ease of application, 2) information value, 3) predictability, and 4) explanatory power.

Ease of Application

In common-sense applications of a theory, the relative **ease of application** depends on the understandability of the theory to the persons using it, and the degree to which the terms and hypotheses of the theory fit the facts of the case under analysis. Social scientists, however, are more likely to go beyond the intuitive and examine the question of **testability** of a theory. It involves the extent to which the variables can be separately and reliably measured by different researchers. If we could not measure the concepts, our theory would not be falsifiable, but rather a tautology or mere opinion. We could not then gather evidence for and against the validity of the hypotheses contained in the theory. A result of testability is the degree to which the theory is productive for those doing research. That is, how fruitful is it in generating *evidence*? Testability also involves the applicability of the theory to real-life events. Ideally, a tested theory should be applicable to policy decisions of administrators, or perhaps to recommendations and therapeutic methodologies of counselors and organizational change agents. Furthermore, a testable hypothesis is methodologically sound. The form of the theory as a whole must be clear, simply or economically stated, complete in application to the events to be explained. It should be elegantly stated as well (Mullins: 1971). Finally, the indicators of each concept of the theory should be observable in a way that will allow us to quantify them. As a final word, it should be clear that for a student who has not yet had a course in social research methods, these points about testability can be safely passed over lightly. He should instead focus simply on the ease of application of the perspectives presented to events and experiences in his own group life.

Information Value

Once we discern that a theory is applicable to the case under consideration, it is natural to look at the criterion of **information value.** Here we ask the questions: How well does the theory help us to describe *what* actually happens, the nature of the events and their sequence? Do the concepts and hypotheses of the theory focus our attention on the meaningful and significant, on facts and solid ideas rather than on mere opinion, the trivial or tautologous? An informative theory is also proximate to *experience* rather than being purely conceptual.

Predictability

The third crucial criterion for judging a theory is its **predictive potential.** Are the variables related in causal or functional statements? Do the statements tell us, for example, that if and when A happens, B will follow? Naturally, if we can predict, then we can more easily control our destiny, or at least set limits to it. Another aspect of prediction is **postdiction,** which is prediction of events occurring at time 2 (after the turning point) from the events or circumstances at time 1 (before the turning point), but making that prediction at a point in time after both time 1 and time 2 events have already transpired, or even where data have already been collected on both points or periods of time. We may be able to predict, however, on the basis of past experience alone, through correlations, even without being able to explain why the prediction held true. This brings us to the fourth, and most important, of the criteria for judging a theory, namely, explanatory power.

Explanatory Power

Explanatory power is the essence of a theory. It tells how well a theory shows *why* there was change or stability in a person or group over a given period of time. More broadly, it tells why what actually happened did in fact occur. Finally, it evaluates how well the hypotheses of the theory order the data, the basic concepts, relationships, and assumptions. Explanation is another word for theory. It goes beyond prediction. Prediction without reasons, without knowledge of conditions, or causes, or motives is a useful happening, but a poor substitute for understanding. If we understand, we will also of course be more able to predict. Thus, with these four criteria, we have a very general but very powerful means of comparing and evaluating all perspectives treated in this text.

UTILITY OF PRESENT STRATEGY

The above four criteria achieve their maximum value when they are used to evaluate the relative utility of two theories at a time, applied to a single case of change over time. When so used, the four criteria can greatly illuminate the general theoretical problem of social science. To repeat in different words, that problem is: *How is a social order changed or reinforced over a period of time?* Or alternatively: *How is joint action originated and sustained in the face of conflict?* Social order, of course, may include international as well as interpersonal relations. On a lower level of abstraction, the practical or social problem may vary from that of troubled relationships between marriage or love partners, to that between boss and worker, between co-workers, between teacher and student; or that of conflicting social class interests, inter-ethnic contact, war between nations, or union-management conflict in industry. When we have finally made such comparison of theories as applied, we can much more readily get a feel for the overall utility of each theory. This is crucial, especially for the beginning student. Such application of pairs of theories to a range of concrete problems will surely help the student to make them his own. Hopefully it will occasionally make a contribution to the solution of real personal and social problems.

We have already stated the bare definitions of the four criteria for a good theory. A closer look at their utility should help to make them a bit more understandable. If a theory or perspective is not easy to apply to concrete situations every researcher or observer will look for different phenomena under the banner of the same theory. A social scientist, as we have seen, looks for measurability or testability. He seeks to find out if a theory is falsifiable, formalized, and whether its concepts are reliably and validly measured. Many other subordinate dimensions could be listed here, but it is important to stick to the most basic and inclusive.

The criterion of information value is useful because no explanation is possible without as far as possible an economical, analytic, rich, exhaustive, inclusive description. It sensitizes us, facilitates reference to live experience, brings the reader closer to the concrete, observable realities of the situation being described. The more the terms and hypotheses of the theory aid us in assimilating information, visualizing the content, and generating insight, the greater will be our understanding of the reality of the situation, or realization of the truth of the matter. Definitiveness is an ideal, but not normally possible in most contemporary research in social science. A good case study usually gives us the best description, especially if the researcher uses many methods of observing, particularly participant observation. The vitality of data gathered in this way is usually quite obvious.

It is interesting to note that the inductive mode of research and theory building produces the highest information value. Some researchers say that detached, yet empathetic immersion in one's theoretical problem and human subject matter is the best way to achieve the goals of research. Valid and vital description is the necessary and primary step to valid conclusions to any study. This is so largely because good description often implies or provides the seeds of an explanation. The more cogent it is, complete in scope, precise and analytical, and the more the description squares with the observations, the better will be the accompanying explanation. Description nevertheless can never be a substitute for explanation.

Predictability is a kind of substantive criterion which is, from one point of view, nonessential in itself. This is so because predictability is subordinate to or a result of being able to explain. Prediction aids us to cope with or to control our environment. Prediction is specific, while its weaker cousin, forecasting, is vague and incomplete. In practice, most student illustrations of theories will inevitably involve postdiction (where the outcome is known ahead of time) rather than prediction, as such. This is so because nearly all introductory students will be employing ready-made stories or personal experience to illustrate a theory for the purpose of learning it and comparing it to other theories. They will not be doing scientific testing.

Finally, what is the utility of explanatory power? Explanation is synonymous with theory. An explanatory theory must be in harmony with other extant explanations. An explanation generalizes about classes of events in the social order. It is a handy, multi-purpose tool, and even an end in itself, a provider of meaning. It makes sense of otherwise unrelated bits of data. It is a possible solution to the theoretical problem which must be at issue in every truly social scientific study. Explanation provides us with causes or reasons or logic. Deductively interrelated statements are essential, necessary, even sufficient conditions for theory. Facts, correlations and tautologies are not substitutes. Principles and evidence are the distinguishing characteristics of social science.

After the student evaluates a situation with a pair of theories or perspectives, he should be cautioned that no explanation is ever *complete and definitive*. This should be obvious anyway, so long as he has taken the task seriously. This caution is in line with the functional mode of theory building (defined above as an evolutionary or gradualist process of interplay between theory and data). For all practical purposes, the functional mode of theory building is in the long run most fruitful for students, and most appropriate for present-day social science. As already noted, it consists in continual revision of theory based on ever better data gathering in successive waves and stages of research. As a final recommendation, the most useful approach to research is more likely to be inductive at the start, but deductive when stated in relatively final form.

CONCLUSION: THE HUMAN MOTIVE FOR SCIENCE

When the concepts of this chapter are put into use in the way proposed in the Preface and Student Use section (after Part II), the applicability of **Social Psychological Theories** to genuinely human problems will readily be seen. When a theory of science is put to use to solve pressing personal and social problems, it is then truly humanistic in the best and most complete sense of the word. But when all is said and done, why do scientists themselves devote their lives to theory and research? Is there a way to bridge the gap between the human and the scientific, the soft and hard-nosed, the tender-minded and tough-minded (W. James: 1907), the cool and warm? (Maslow: 1966). The approach of this volume is open to either style. Perhaps we can join Abraham Maslow to obtain "religious" experiences, a sense of mystery, or peak experiences from scientific reading and research. Perhaps with Carl Rogers (1961) we can carry on research or construct theory because it is satisfying to perceive the world as having order and meaning. Rogers further states:

> I have almost invariably found that the very feeling which has seemed to me most private, most personal, and hence most incomprehensible by others, has turned out to be an expression for which there is a resonance in many other people. It has led me to believe that what is most personal and unique in each one of us is probably the very element which would, if it were shared or expressed, speak most deeply to others. This has helped me to understand artists and poets as people who have dared to express the unique in themselves (1961: p. 26).

Most students who are likely to read this book, no matter what their major interests, will probably concur with Rogers, and Maslow, and Nisbet (1962) that there is no intrinsic contradiction between science and humanism. Certainly, a theory that does not provide aesthetic enjoyment is less attractive to us as fully human persons. How can we really keep from being "turned on" by the one, the true, the good and the beautiful? For our long-run satisfaction, we will need to understand the concepts of social science, and the prevailing trend to quantitatively verify and qualify commonly known hypotheses. But for our ultimate as well as our immediate purpose, such concepts and data are mere stepping-stones to discovery of the exciting social world around us.

SUMMARY OF APPROACH OF WHOLE TEXT

By way of review of this section, as well as a preview of the overall technique used in this handbook, the following abstract of the author's basic approach is presented. This procedural summary indicates the major methodological contribution of the handbook as a whole.

Demonstration of Hypotheses

My technique can be used to illustrate any social scientific hypothesis, perspective, or concept. My *teaching objective* is to systematically demonstrate or concretely *apply* abstract social scientific ideas by means of progressive schedules of *reinforcement* of them, and in the process emphasize a) student initiative and participation, b) some teaching *by* students, c) evaluation of the theory as applied, especially d) in terms of four criteria for a good theory. Helpful materials include a resource box with catalogs of films, simulation games, *Handbook of Structured Experiences for Human Relations Training*, plot outlines of plays and novels (e.g., in *Masterplots*), and scenes from theater plays (e.g., in *Great Scenes from the World Theater*, 2 volumes).

The *procedure* includes at least six steps:
1.   For each theory, as introduced, *list* half a dozen concepts and three central hypotheses on chalkboard by way of *preview*.
2.   Give a *mini-lecture* on the theory.
3.   Students type an *abstract* of the theory (50-200 words).
4.   Instructor or reader grades and comments on abstracts within one week's time.
5.   Later, each student takes one or two theories as a whole (e.g., symbolic interactionism and exchange theory) and systematically *illustrates* it (in 3-5 pages, according to a careful format sheet) using auto/biographical material, a scene from a

theater play, a novel, film, or any written fiction. Then he evaluates each theory *with reasons and examples* for his rating on the four criteria for a good theory, namely, ease of application of the theory for this story or example, which involves testability in part; information value (including range and descriptiveness of the concepts); predictability (of the theory for the main change or sequence of events described); and explanatory power (or how well the theory tells why the main person or group changed or remained the same over time). The four criteria are evaluated as the student has applied the theory to the story plot. This requires that the student first pick out the main person or group being analyzed, stating the initial situation at time 1 (before), the intervening event (causing change), time 2 (outcome after the change). Also, hypotheses should be stated to try to explain change over time in a person or a group. (A full example of this evaluation is available in my paper on "Evaluating Theories Comparatively"[1] and can also be found in this handbook.)

6.   Still later, to get a grade of A or B, students work in pairs to give an *oral demonstration* of two theories at a time. Each student/organizer/facilitator/demonstrator states and illustrates one hypothesis from his chosen separate theory based on the common oral presentation, which may be a sociodrama, simulation game, film, dramatic reading of a play scene (but not offhand or partial or separate examples for each concept or hypothesis). A *debriefing* sesson follows the demonstration proper. This oral demonstration as a whole should be set up to be followed by the *main purpose*, namely, to generate *discussion*, preferably in small groups. Best format for discussion sequence is the "funnel" technique of questioning, namely, from general to particular. Each group writes joint answers to each question for discussion, to be turned in at end of class and signed by each participant.

Possible pitfalls include the need for full instruction, step-by-step, with a notebook of examples done by previous students, or dry-runs for the orals. It is best to offer students the option to rewrite any paper to raise an undesirable grade. The technique can be used for any course. I have used it most often in social psychology, contemporary theory, the family, and social organization.

---

[1]Published in Zeitschrift für Soziologie, 3, 4, October 1974, 397–408.

Part I

HUMANISTIC-DEVELOPMENTAL THEORIES

These two perspectives (social actualization and identity development) are presented first because they set the stage for freeing our minds and emotions for new and deeper insights into human social behavior through a lifetime. This basic attitude of freedom is required before the student of society and people can see and feel more clearly what is going on around him. It seems natural to begin with these basically *psychological* approaches, since by tradition and upbringing we are almost always taught that the person is the cornerstone of society, the cloth of social fabric, the one morally responsible, and the one alone who can ultimately create a better life for himself and all mankind. If this seems to be a truism, let it be challenged here and now. An important *sociological* view is that the whole is greater than the sum of its parts. There are many elements of group behavior that cannot be examined by concepts describing individuals. For example, how can anyone validly describe group integration, esprit de corps, leadership, reciprocity between persons, or communication, or conformity to group standards without simultaneous consideration of the characteristics of both members and the group as a whole?

Pedagogically, it seems most provocative if we begin our study of social psychology by looking first at what is most interesting, personal, and meaningful to most students or most thoughtful lay people, nonscientists and nonprofessionals. Then a bit later we need to broaden our scope and viewpoint to wider and often more abstract sociological dimensions. In the opinion of this writer, the most provocative and immediately real, vital, and direct approach to personal problems and relationships that is academically relevant is the school of humanistic psychology (treated in Chapter 1 as social actualization). While many scholars and social scientists would quarrel with the value of humanistic psychology, others have devoted their lives to it. Furthermore, the contemporary wish for a return to the self and to one's peer group is seen in the movement of thousands of Westerners toward meditation, Yoga, Eastern modes of thought, togetherness, sensitivity groups, environmental purification and recycling of raw material and energy, the radical student, the Third World, as well as the futurist movement. Members of all these movements can exchange lessons with the humanistic social scientists. Thus we are beginning this book with what is most concrete, meaningful, and understandable to youth on the frontiers of thought and action.

In such fashionable movements, however, there is a danger in focusing too narrowly on separate individuals or on oneself. The result may be isolationism or egoism, or worse, a lack of consciousness or interest in the social, economic, governmental, and educational patterns that make it possible for the underprivileged and deprived masses to share the benefits of a better life. Maslow's need ladder (see Chapter 1) raises the question of needs for love and affection. But clearly these needs cannot be fulfilled unless others are willing and able to give it. And we are much less likely to receive unless we give in kind. The developmental idea of stages of human needs is contained in the five steps of Maslow's need ladder. Eight alternate stages of man are contained in Erikson's neo-Freudian descriptions of eight age groupings in human life (Chapter 2). Both approaches have been used in counseling. Erikson's perspective is rather heavily psychoanalytic. Maslow's perspective is more broadly inclusive without restricting itself to particular concepts or sequences of events.

We are beginning then with a background of these two theories, social actualization, and identity development. One focuses on deeper human needs and emotionally relevant concepts, the other on needs as developed through a lifetime. With the introduction of these two basic perspectives, the stage will be set to raise at least one absolutely crucial question and one parallel but subordinate question of all succeeding theories, namely: How can this theory help us as individuals to achieve *self-actualization?* And subordinately: How can this theory help us to achieve *social actualization,* or a better society?

Chapter 1

Social Actualization

In the past few years, some far-sighted and deep-thinking scholars have reacted against the dominance of academic psychology by behavioristic or quantitatively oriented laboratory researchers. They have become interested in studying the hard but important questions, as well as in directly experiencing the deeper values of social life. They call themselves humanistic psychologists. Their interest is in freedom, hope, love, and even ESP (extrasensory perception), mystical and parapsychological experiences, with a goal of self-actualization, or personal fulfillment. Without rejecting basic scientific methods, they are striving to put deeper needs, interests, and values in human perspective. Their methods are often introspective, and almost always qualitative.

Maslow's need ladder is perhaps the most central partial theory representative of this **social actualization** tradition. The need ladder gives us an extremely helpful view of the potential for individual self development. It consists of five stages. Each stage must be mastered to a sufficient degree by satisfying our most basic needs for **survival,** such as food, clothing, and shelter. After these needs are reasonably satisfied we can then give our attention largely to satisfying our needs for **security and safety,** e.g., freedom from personal attack, etc. When these previous needs are sufficiently satisfied, we can develop our capacity for **love and affection.** Then we are in a position to satisfy our need for attaining **esteem of self and others.** Finally, we can achieve some degree of **self-actualization,** at least for a given period of time.

Ordinarily we do not have enough energy for more than a limited number of "peak experiences." These experiences indicate that for that moment we are participating in that occasional state of existence which we call self-actualization. It is a state which few people enjoy for any extended period of time, least of all as a way of life. Yet it is the goal of practically every human being to achieve it in one form or another. It is something akin to the achievement of the Yogis and mystics, a consciousness of personal goals as well as a personal recognition of the path and process of getting there. This does not mean only or exclusively a *rational* self-consciousness. It may only require an *intuitive* sense of direction in life, and a sense of how to prepare oneself to live life to the fullest, depending of course on one's unique personality and living circumstances. The emotional element is strong in this state. It is understood that one cannot achieve happiness by any exclusively rational process. We can at best only prepare the way for the joyful life. Then its achievement may or may not come. But if it does, it is a gift and a surprise, and for that reason all the more joyful.

Although their goal is noble, even the humanistic psychologists frequently overlook ideas of the "good society," of the need for understanding and work towards social actualization alongside the psychological or self-actualization. After all, we are predominantly social beings. We are bounded largely by our social environment. If it is difficult to research and understand human personalities or societies separately, it is more difficult yet to understand them *together*, in context. It is hard enough to do this philosophically. It is harder still to do it social scientifically. But together is indeed the way we experience personalities and society in our everyday living. Society and self are but two sides of a coin (Cooley). Yet we cannot understand the coin by looking at only one side.

One example of the meaning of social actualization (a term of the author's invention) is that experience and sense of community felt between goods friends, between members of a close-knit family, team, or religious community. It is the opposite of that sense of alienation felt by most people in their relations with fellow citizens of large cities in our future-shocked, technologized, bureaucratized world. (On this point see "The Experience of Living in Cities," by Milgram.)

Examples

■ Peak experiences which indicate the attainment of self-actualization might be as varied as the feeling of a cool breeze on a hot summer night on the porch; a kiss from a lover; a mountain climber's first panoramic view of the wooded valley and snow-capped mountains after arriving at the peak; a mother hearing the cry of her newborn baby; a shimmering purple sunset over the ocean casting up its rays onto a mackerel-clouded sky; a joyous reunion with an old friend; children gleefully opening their presents under the Christmas tree. All these are moments which can hardly be planned and rationally achieved. We can only prepare the way by gradually ascending the previous four steps of the need ladder. It is left for a future theorist, or perhaps better for the artist or the poet to show us how to better prepare, how to move a step higher up the ladder. Once we have experienced such a peak, hardly any further motivation is needed to seek to repeat it. It is our dilemma as human beings that we cannot maintain such a state as though in suspended animation. We must be ever searching, and follow the soft inner voice that leads the way in our career through life.

Going a step further, the attempt to help others to achieve self-actualization or to facilitate their "trip" is liable to lead to a deep relationship with them, a love, or friendship which in itself is the best possible example of the attainment of social actualization. A brother who helps a brother feels no burden. And when that brotherhood spans nationality and culture, there is hope for a world of peace. Such may happen between a dedicated public servant and the acclaim of his fellow citizens. It may happen between diplomats at a peace conference between Arabs and Israeli, in the United Nations, in racially integrated schools, in the Peace Corps, or among students in an international exchange program. The goal is so simple it can be appreciated by every person who thinks a bit more deeply about the world. But the goal is at once so lofty that as members of the human race we must honestly say that only the heroes among us have begun to take the first steps. ■

Our hope is that by introducing this perspective first the student will be motivated to look for hints of ways to attain self and social actualization in each of the remaining fifteen perspectives presented in this book. Some very brief attempts to glean such insights are presented at the end of the Critique of each of the sixteen perspectives presented after the five parts. Again the actualization perspective was presented first because it seems to be more interesting and potentially personally important to more students. And finally, in our opinion, it emphasizes what is most lacking in most other contemporary social psychological theories, namely, humanistic values.

See *Recommended Reading* section, beginning on page 143, as well as the *Study Questions* for this chapter beginning on page 144 of the Appendix.

The student should now do a *50-Word Summary* followed by a *Three-Page Write-Up* illustrating this social actualization perspective by relating it to his own life or that of some close friend. See instructions for doing these tasks at the end of Part I, on pages 30–38. A sample is also given of such a write-up done by a student on the perspective of actualization.

Chapter 2

Identity Development
(Neo-Freudian Socialization)

Identity development is less a unique theory than a perspective that looks at the major stages of personal change through a lifetime of social development. Lesser, shorter-term changes (e.g., changes of people within a given age group or a given developmental stage) can be explained by the so-called "micro" level theories (such as S-R behaviorism, exchange, cognitive dissonance, and group dynamics) which the reader will see later in the handbook. Yet important aspects of life will be glossed over by such narrowly focused theories unless they are accompanied by and hung on the tree of a global perspective like identity development. (The title for this perspective is again unique to the author.) Most thinkers in this area of human development have focused on childhood and its developmental tasks. Havighurst (1953), for example, lists some nine tasks for adolescents between twelve and eighteen years of age, such as accepting one's physique and a masculine or feminine role, emotional independence of parents and other adults, selecting and preparing for an occupation, for marriage and civic competence. Others have focused on the stages of moral development (e.g., Piaget and Kohlberg), or on the strength of the relationship between socializer and socializee (Maccoby: 1968). Adult socialization processes have only recently come of interest among social scientists (Brim and Wheeler: 1966).

Erik Erikson, however, is undoubtedly the most important thinker in this area owing to his pioneering work, his consideration of the eight stages of development from infancy to a mature age, each with its corresponding major task. Although his focus is on the development of identity in adolescence, he views the order of development of characteristic virtues or strengths or accomplishments at certain age levels as follows:

The person must achieve a certain degree of mastery of the problem of trust in others before developing his separate autonomy, and a certain sufficient degree of autonomy before initiative, etc., through the eight stages, hopefully ending in integrity at a late age in the normal person's life. If the individual does not achieve sufficient mastery at a given stage, or skips a task, he will subsequently be forced or required by circumstances to return psychologically at some later (chronological) time in order to develop that skipped developmental virtue. He must also learn to handle the failure or opposite virtues at each stage, namely, mistrust, shame or doubt, guilt, etc., because these problems are virtually unavoidable in a meaningful and active life. In a more recent book (entitled *Adulthood*) Erikson suggests more explicitly that if conditions are favorable, when the characteristic virtue dominates over the recurring problem at each stage, a new strength emerges. The eight new strengths are: hope, will, purpose, competence, fidelity, love, care, and wisdom.

The central step is the achievement by the person of a sense of psychosocial identity, a sense of who he is, where he has been, and where he is going. The identity crisis is central to Erikson's developmental theory. It is a major turning point in the person's emotional life in which there are usually signs of identity diffusion, which may include the inability to concentrate, excessive awareness, inability to work, to exercise, to get along with people, a "formless fantasy" or persistent anxiety.

Stage (Age)	Developmental Virtue	Vs. Opposite Problem
1. Infancy (1)	Trust	Mistrust
2. Early Childhood (2–3)	Autonomy	Shame, Doubt
3. Play Age (4–5)	Initiative	Guilt
4. School Age (6–11)	Industry	Inferiority
5. Adolescence (12–18)	Identity	Identity Diffusion, Role Confusion
6. Young Adult	Intimacy	Isolation
7. Adulthood (through Middle Age)	Generativity	Self-absorption
8. Mature Age	Integrity	Disgust, Despair

Examples

■ It would require analysis of an entire lifetime of a person to give a complete example of the eight stages of the perspective. In the absence of such complete information, we must usually restrict ourselves to shorter periods of time, to portions of a lifetime, or to particular concepts. However, the life of Mahatma Gandhi embodied the eight characteristics as much as any one who ever lived. Gandhi had an abundant trust in his people and his fellow man as seen in the many risks he took to free his Indian pople from British rule. His marches and demonstrations of passive resistance often laid him open to danger of physical retaliation by armed authorities and extremist or fanatical antagonists. He overcame the mistrust of countless enemies. He was trusting to his death, slain by an assassin's bullet. He certainly maintained his autonomy as a separate person. He even reduced his total belongings to what he could easily carry with him independent of any other person. His initiative was so great that practically single-handedly he founded the movement for Indian independence. His industry carried the movement to its goal after long years of work. He achieved unquestionable identity as a person with a mission in life of promoting political freedom and religious values and truth. But he certainly had identity crises along the way, as a husband at age 13; as a shy and lonely law student in England; as a meek, nonviolent activist and outspoken protestor against imperialist injustices in his homeland of India, with all the accompanying anxieties. And he did come out of these crises by confirming his self-concept. He achieved intimacy outside his own family not only with his wife, but with diplomats and friends throughout the world. The generativity of his adult working life came as a lawyer and political organizer and originator of an idea that increased the productivity and human fulfillment of countless numbers of his countrymen, the use of the spinning wheel. He was certainly a man of integrity who looked back humbly at the diverse experiences of his life which he fit together with a philosophy of truth, altruism, asceticism, and freedom. ■

See *Recommended Reading* section and *Study Questions*, beginning on page 145. The student is encouraged here to do a *50-Word Summary* plus a *Three-Page Write-Up* applying identity development to his own life or that of a close friend. See instructions for the summary plus the illustrative write-up on pages 30–38.

Critique of Humanistic-Developmental Theories

REVIEW AND COMPARISON

The reader should here reread the summaries of the first two perspectives contained in the introductions to Chapters 1 and 2. It does not seem possible yet to synthesize these two approaches into a unified whole. But we can easily see the similarities by comparing the five steps of the need ladder to the eight stages of human development. We can see that when our physical needs for **survival** are satisfied (Maslow), then we can begin to **trust** (Erikson) as we satisfy our needs for **security** and **safety** (Maslow). We can in turn become more **autonomous,** take **initiative,** show **industry,** develop **identity** (Erikson). Identity (Erikson) seems closest to, though one step below, Maslow's need for **esteem** of self and others. Maslow's need for **love** and **affection** seems closest to Erikson's **intimacy.** Thus, the original order of these last two pairs of terms is reversed from one theory to the other. Continuing in chronological order of development, there follows **generativity** and **integrity** (Erikson's terms), and finally **self-actualization** (Maslow). It should be noted that self-actualization can be attained within at least the later of the eight stages of man, though the form of the actualization experience will of course vary at each stage. What remains for future theorizing is to explain the mechanisms and processes whereby a person advances from one step or stage to the next. Also, what are some guidelines for counseling a person who has either skipped a step or seems unable to move on either to the next step or ultimately to self-actualization? Thirdly, how can one recognize whether he has attained each characteristic virtue or ultimate self-actualization? What are the practical, observable criteria? These are some of the searching questions which every sincere student must inevitably ask himself about every serious theory or policy or life-style he encounters.

Evaluation and Application of Social Actualization

Social actualization is a highly inductive perspective, because it usually starts with observational data, and develops theory out of the data. This theory is then open to deductive elaboration in future studies. Its employment of highly value-laden concepts means that its ease of application to research comes only after a struggle, at least in most instances. Once it is applied, and depending as always on the particular application, it can be highly informative. However, it is generally quite lacking in the explicit hypotheses required to aid prediction and unambiguous explanation. It remains nevertheless highly insightful. Empirical support for actualization is wanting despite a great deal of interest in the approach in very recent years among social scientists.

To change a person using insights from social actualization, we would help him become aware of his potential for fulfilling himself, by discussion, dialogue, and pertinent experience. Presumably he could be made to see that what we want him to do is a stepping-stone to, or even a part of, his ladder to self- and social actualization.

Examples

■ A teacher, a parent, and a friend all have their task of challenging and giving rise to what is noble in a person. They will want to help a person to grow, to realize what is best in him. But they will not do it in a way that imposes their views, but through genuine communication and deep dialogue which urges him to his personally chosen manner and life goal. Such a contribution to a person's ideal is surely unlikely to be monetary, but rather intimate, personal, even so subtle as to be unrecognized. A pat on the back at the right moment; a serious conversation and advice about choices for a fulfilling career; valuable time and energy freely given; all these are the little extras that will change another person without controlling him. Such simple deeds will become contagious and may even change and actualize mankind. ■

The actualization perspective in itself contains no formal theory of how to attain self-actualization, step-by-step. Rather, it prefers to leave this open to individual personal needs and meta-urges as experienced and intuited.

Example

■ Attainment comes from patiently preparing the way, setting the stage for advancement up the need ladder. And once the step of love and affection is entered, the only real way to receive is to give in kind, even without expecting a return. If that is done, then the love received from others is unexpected, more of a surprise, and more likely to be a peak experience, a self-actualizing moment. The way is prepared in moments of solitude, reflective meditation and sensing of what is best and finest in the long run for ourselves as fully human beings, contributors to a world of peace and harmony. ■

Evaluation and Application of Identity Development

Identity development as a perspective was developed inductively because the theory evolved out of Erikson's clinical observations and data. Although it had been developed in a reasonably systematic way (by Erik Erikson in his eight stages of man), it was and continues to be used in a deductive manner to generate new testable hypotheses. It applies easily to lifelong case studies, but tends to quickly fall short when applied to shorter periods of time within a person's life span. This is obvious because the eight ages span a lifetime. When it does apply, it has moderately good predictability for many circumstances; for example, if one fails to develop the characteristic virtue of the given age, say initiative at age 4–5, he will have problems with initiative later in life, at least until that virtue is sufficiently developed. Information value and explanatory power in these circumstances are also very high. It not only helps characterize the person's emotional focus at each stage, but gives a reason why crises occur. (Note that these judgments of relative utility are based purely on the experience of the author and his students in applying all theories of this book to many concrete situations. Naturally these judgments will vary from one student to the next.) Empirical support for identity development is rather limited since it requires such long-term career data and case material.

   To change a person with identity development, change his socializers or significant others. If you are one of them, use your influence to help him attain the characteristic trait of his next stage of development. To change him in a particular way, help to fit the kind of behavior we want him to engage in into his scheme of life seen at his present and next stage of development. Show him how it will help him to achieve identity and ultimate integrity. If our wish for him does not fit, or blocks his movement through the stages, it would only be counterproductive to try to get him to do it.

Example

■   There are certain typical delinquent types noted in the literature (Gibbons:1965) which follow a career pattern. Although we would like to think that the women's liberation movement has changed all this, it is still the case that young women commit different types of delinquent offenses than do boys. The typical "female delinquent" often becomes so as a consequence of inadequate affectional relationships in the family. She substitutes affection with boys. Sexual favors are given in return for affection. She becomes an "easy lay," and a vicious circle of problems follows. Hostility and "tough" characteristics form a protective outer shell for her poor affectional relations. To change such a person, identity development would direct us to examine her sense of identity as a person and need for intimacy. Treatment agencies frequently commit such a girl to a training school if probation does not help (which may not be endorsed by Erikson). There she will deal intimately with peers in a cottage situation. Normal maturation processes take effect in most cases. Group therapy often seems to help to take a realistic view of her past experiences, especially regarding hostility to parents. Family therapy would be ideal, if feasible, to help achieve greater intimacy where it was originally lacking. In most cases, the female delinquent achieves identity stability in the role as a wife in her own family in somewhat later years.   ■

To achieve self-actualization with identity development, we must try to move gradually through the stages of development in appropriate order with a view to developing our capacities and inner being to the fullest at each stage. The specifics of how to go about this are unstated. Future research should direct itself to clarifying this point.

Example

■   The liberated woman, in the best sense of the word, is one who has learned to establish equal and democratic relationships with men on a personal and occupational level. She would necessarily have to have developed a rather high degree of the eight characteristics of the *integrally* developed person. A unique, liberated **identity** should allow her to take a fuller measure of **initiative** in her life than the average woman. The result should be greater **generativity** in the nonfamily world of work. The reverse side of the coin here is that a truly liberated woman can more easily accept the expression of tender emotions on the part of her male friends. Men, in turn, are allowed a larger measure of **intimacy,** with hopefully a freer flowing communication and a higher level of **self-** and **social actualization** as a result. ■

STUDENT USE INSTRUCTIONS[1]

50-Word Summary

It is extremely useful and important for each student to write his own summary for each theory immediately after he encounters it. These summaries should be carefully done and then corrected by the teacher or reader for the course, and then if necessary revised by the student. This is an excellent aid to the memory, not to mention the understanding. Further, such summaries provide an excellent guide for review and later reference in future courses taken by the student. Some may object by saying that this sounds like busywork. But only someone who has not tried the assignment is likely to say that. Instructions for such an assignment follow.

A. Type or print legibly in ink on 4 × 6 (or larger) cards.
    I.   List only the key concepts of the perspective, in logical order.
        A.   Define the new or difficult concepts.
           1)   Eliminate nonessential concepts and complexity.
    II. Use a table, or diagram the relationship between the key concepts if traditional or possible to do so.
    III. The primary task here is as follows: Describe how change or reinforced commitment from time 1 (= before) to time 2 (= after some crucial event) in a person or group can be explained using this perspective.
        A.   With a more in-depth discussion, show how either 1) changes, or 2) a matrix of conditions, or 3) a

---

[1] The following several pages, pp. 31–33, may be skipped or skimmed by the reader who is uninterested in these suggested pedagogical exercises. If time is available, however, doing these exercises is probably the most effective way of making the theories your own. Nevertheless, it would still be useful at least to read the sample application paper written by a former student in the author's course, on pp. 34–37.

> relationship of variables in the original social or
> personality structures at time 1 can be used 1) to
> predict, or at least 2) to describe and 3) explain the
> conditions of the same structure(s) at a later period or
> point in time (= time 2).

The summary should be self-contained, i.e., understandable by an intelligent reader not previously familiar with the perspective treated. Otherwise, write it in such a way that the instructor will be able to see that you understand the essence of the perspective after one quick reading of your summary.

You might want to give an example on the back of the card for your own future reference. But it is better to avoid examples in the 50-word summary itself. Instead, you should spend more time sharpening, simplifying, and seeing to it that your summary is accurate and complete on the essential items or concepts of the perspective. It is more important to be terse and accurate than to worry about the exact number of words in the summary.

Instructions for Everyday Application

The Three-Page Write-Ups

The next step in bringing home the practicality of a theory is to apply the careful, abstract (50-Word Summary) statement to a concrete case either in the life of the student or a friend, or to some film or stage play, or short story or biography, etc. This can be done in three double-spaced typed pages. One theory can be applied point-by-point, concept-by-concept, hypothesis-by-hypothesis to a single sequence of events showing change over time in a person or a group. This should be followed by an evaluation of your application with reasons for each rating on the four criteria for a good theory: 1) ease of application, 2) information value, 3) predictability, and 4) explanatory power.

Equivalent specific instructions for such an *Everyday Application* are given after Part IV (for cognitive dissonance). The following instructions may be used for illustrating one or two theories at a time. If you intend to illustrate only one theory, simply omit only those items that are concerned with the second theory. Let us be fully explicit about each step. This assignment consists in applying the key elements of one or two perspectives at a time to one concrete sequence of events. Comparison of two perspectives is an extremely useful device for understandng the relative merit of one theory in relation to another. Very detailed instructions are given in order to aid the student in carefully ordering his ideas. The uniform style of presentation is also necessary where an instructor must read a very large number of papers.

The task is to illustrate and evaluate the relative utility of one or two major social psychological perspectives in three double-spaced typed pages. Illustrate both perspectives by applying their main points to some factual, real-life, or written fictional story. Do not fabricate a story, nor merely give an example off the top of your head. Find a story or experience with enough explicit detail. Here is a list of some useful sources:

1.   A drama, movie, novel, or short story giving depth of character or detail about a relationship or individual in a group, such as the works of G. B. Shaw, Eugene O'Neill, or William Shakespeare.
2.   A story from some news magazine or newspaper.
3.   Some article from *Psychology Today,* or *Society Today.*
4.   Some article from an advice column, such as Ann Landers or Joyce Brothers, etc., if enough detail is given. (It usually is not.)
5.   Some real, living individual whom you know very well who has undergone some significant change or commitment.

This person could be yourself. You are your own best example. For best results, choose a story or sequence of events in real life that involves some crucial decision or turning point taken by an individual (or possibly by a small group) involving some change in behavior patterns, or some notable affirmation of commitment to the status quo by the initiating party (protagonist or main actor or group). The write-up itself should include the following items, preferably by number and letter.

I.   Briefly (in under 50 words) summarize the story, stating the two periods or points in time and the nature of the intervening crucial event or turning point. State the source of your story, whether it is a personal autobiography, or written fiction. If the source is fiction, be sure to include the author, date, title, source, pages, etc.
II.   Summarize your first chosen perspective in under 50 words, preferably in the form of concise hypotheses. Underline key concepts.
III.   Apply this first perspective to your story, step-by-step.
  A.   Note changes in behavior patterns or commitment from time 1 (before) to time 2 (after the crucial event) on each of the key variables (or concepts in your hypotheses). Underline key concepts as you go.

    B. Explain or state why the change in behavior or reaffirmed commitment came about, based on this perspective.

(If you are doing a write-up of only one theory, skip to item VI.)

IV. Summarize your second chosen perspective in under 50 words, preferably in the form of hypotheses. Underline key concepts.

 V. Apply this second chosen perspective to your story, step-by-step.

    A. Note changes in behavior patterns or commitment from time 1 (before) to time 2 (after the crucial event) on each of the key variables contained in your hypotheses. Underline the key concepts as you go.

    B. Explain or state why the change in behavior or reaffirmed commitment came about, based on this perspective.

VI. Evaluate the utility of your perspective(s) as you have applied it (them) to your story. Use the following crucial comparative dimensions, giving reasons for your rating, and a terse example for your evaluation. They are:

    A. Ease of application (this may involve testability of the hypotheses with your data, though it usually will not)

    B. Information value

    C. Predictability, or predictive potential

    D. Explanatory power

The student would do well to carefully reread the passages of the introductory chapter to this volume for definitions of these four dimensions. A further example of their use-in-practice is given in the *Sample Comparative Write-Ups*. One such sample immediately follows. Others are given at the ends of Parts II, IV, and V. An example of a write-up using only one theory was given after Chapter 1 on actualization. This evaluation portion of the assignment is essential to show your understanding in practice. You may include the original story or clipping if you like. But your summary (item I) and your application (items III and V above) must be self-contained, i.e., readable without the whole original story.

SAMPLE STUDENT WRITE-UP

This illustration follows the format on pages 31–33 in the text.

ACTUALIZATION

January 10, 1972
Social Psychology
Allen M. Johnson

I. Summary of Story. I will review my childhood and youth
and some tribulations as a prelude to a revelation which has
given greater meaning and mission to my later life.
II. Summary of Theory. Actualization theory is treated here
from the point of view of A. H. Maslow's need ladder which is
very basic in humanistic psychology. There are at least five
sets of strengths, virtues, or goals, which are called basic
needs. These are: physiological, security and safety, love
and affection, esteem of self and others and
self—actualization. These basic virtues are related to each
other in a hierarchy of prepotency in the order listed. The
presently most prepotent goal will monopolize
consciousness and will tend of itself to organize the
recruitment of the various capacities of the individual.
When a need is fairly well satisfied, the next higher need
emerges, in turn to dominate. One may fall back or regress
to earlier stages at times. Many never reach the top step.
Occasional peak experiences or ''highs'' may be one
indication of partial attainment of self—actualization.
Self—actualization is the sense of fulfillment or
reasonable satisfaction of one's most basic needs, goals,
values in life, including use of one's talents. Social
actualization is the attainment of the good society for each
of its members.
III. Apply Story. To express the concept of actualization
here is an abbreviated biography of myself. Time 1, the
before in my life, is the time before my revelation.
      I was born on a farm four miles outside of Clarksville,
Texas, June 28, 1915. My parents were middle—class farmers.
They owned their own farm, about 140 acres. They raised
cotton and corn, and planted a garden. In addition to six
head of mules and about a dozen cows, they owned a Model—T
Ford as a family car.

My mother was a high-school graduate. My father got to
the third grade before he was pulled out of school to work.
He admits that my mother taught him how to read. Both
parents came from well-to-do families. My mother's family
was inclined toward higher education in that several of her
brothers and sisters graduated from college, while my
father's family exercised less appreciation for higher
education, but were proud and ambitious.

All of my early childhood needs for <u>security</u> were well
satisfied. At an early age my mother gave me some goals in
life. She wanted me to be like my ''Uncle man,'' who was a
great Baptist preacher, in the class with Billy Sunday for
the Negro. I was encouraged to go to school. My mother was
very close to me because I was the only boy with two sisters.

I was trained to work on my father's farm and it was fun
to me. But working on the farm never got in the way of my
schooling. All of our <u>physical</u> needs were well satisfied. So
was my <u>security and safety</u>.

My mother died when I was fifteen, just two years before
I finished high school. This did not prevent me from
finishing high school, because my father was very
cooperative and insisted that I continue. My chance for
college was made very precarious. As I approached the time,
conditions were more against me because the depression of
the '30s was on. Nevertheless I was determined to go. The
year after I graduated from high school I dropped out and
worked a year with my father on the farm to earn enough money
for school. He gave me a little patch of cotton to finance my
first year, but the cotton prices were down. When I had
gathered it, all I had was $26.00 and my fare to Wiley
College. I went down there hoping that my determination
would see me through. In spite of all my efforts my health
broke and I could not play football. And because of extreme
poverty I was forced to leave. My father could not help me at
all. And because his second wife of 28 days died, he asked me
to come home. I borrowed $5.00 from the president of the
college and returned home. I helped him to make one more
crop and it was a complete failure. I was forced to look
elsewhere for employment, and I was lucky enough to get in
the Soil Conservation Corps as an enrollee. This gave me
some degree of <u>safety and security,</u> and I was able to help
the whole family.

Now I am able to move into another need of my life, the
need for <u>love and affection.</u> This need comes after the

physiological and safety need and was fairly well
gratified. I wanted now to have someone of my own. I wanted a
wife. So I got married in 1940. It was a secret marriage
because as a private in the Army I was not allowed to get
married. While in the CCC I got an opportunity to volunteer
for the Army and I joined.

After a couple of years I began to move up the rank
ladder. This gave me more security and some esteem of self
and others. I now had a desire to obtain a more stable and
firm base, and get a higher evaluation of myself. I climbed
the rank ladder and was finally promoted to the rank of
second lieutenant after finishing OCS.

Life went on and years went by. I had reached the gate of
the last need, self-actualization: What a man can be, he
must be.

I could not feel completely satisfied spiritually. My
life was full of obligations. I was doing things, but I felt
somewhat empty and lost within myself. I began to search and
reevaluate my circumstances. I found many things wrong. My
love life broke down, and I had to give it serious attention
again. Finally I divorced my wife and remarried. This was a
big lift and I began to feel that I could live again. I
continued to search, because my spiritual need and the need
for self-actualization had not yet been satisfied.

Self-actualization finally began to become a reality in
a most unusual way. Here is the crucial event or turning
point in my life. The story runs as follows:

I was stationed in Hawaii in about 1960. I was with my
unit on maneuvers on the island of Hawaii, on top of the
mountain Pohocolo. On top of this mountain we had our base
camp from which we went out every day on field problems and
returned at night to rest. This evening I retired to my bed
about 8:30 p.m. My bed was under a light which was on. The
officers were milling around and playing cards or what have
you. I seemed to have dropped off in a trance suddenly.
While in this state I saw a man dressed in a white robe. He
was very saintly looking with long hair. He beckoned for me
to come toward him. He kept moving backward and beckoning
with arm gestures for me to follow him. He did not say a
word, yet with signs he forcefully indicated that I should
follow. I was anxious and wanted to follow, and suddenly I
was awakened. The lights were still on in the barracks and I
looked at my watch and saw that I had been lying down only
about fifteen minutes. I was quite excited and astonished. I

got up, dressed, and went to the nearest telephone and
called my wife and told her the story. Of course we
discussed some implications. What followed was that she
told a friend nurse of hers and the nurse told her husband
about it. When I returned home some weeks later they invited
me to their church.

At this point, time 2 in my life began. It still
continues.

When I investigated the church it turned out to be a
Mormon Church. I continued to investigate and before I was
baptised I had a repeat of the vision. This made me sure that
I should join. Since that time I have been happy with my
religious life. The problem with the church is, it has a
segregation policy. I know that the church is very wrong and
I speak out against it. I feel someday I will have a hand in
changing the church policy about segregation. This will be
my contribution to social actualization, though I do other
public service work, including work for the poor with the
NAACP. I know that I have not reached the satisfying stage
of actualization, but I am working on it.

(Parts IV and V of the format sheet apply only to use of
2 theories at a time.)

VI. Evaluate Your Application of the Theory.

My progress through the five steps was easily visible,
probably because of the unusual events and sometimes
hardships of my youth. The theory was easy to apply.

The theory had above average information value for my
life's progress because it helped me to briefly describe the
major events and turning points in my career.

The early steps of the need ladder did not help to
predict my revelation. No theory could. Nor did the events
of my youth, except my parents' aspirations, really help to
forecast my social activism and basic self-confidence.

The theory of actualization has helped me to explain
pretty well why I had reached a state of reasonable
self-esteem, and why I am still striving to open the doors
of self and social actualization through advancing work to
achieve my revealed mission in life.[1]

---

[1] During the summer of 1978, Allen Johnson was ordained a priest by the
Mormon Church in Texas.

This example was expanded by the student in more detail than necessary for the assignment. It could easily be shortened to three double-spaced typed pages in order to follow the format sheet. However, it was left in present form in order to retain its human interest value.

Part II

STRUCTURE AND CHANGE THEORIES

This second cluster of perspectives can best be seen as variations on the themes of social structure and social change. They deal with the patterning of relationships in groups both large and small, as well as the processes of changing these patterns. All three perspectives to be introduced here are somewhat fragmentary when matched against the ideal of deductive or axiomatic theory. In part, these perspectives may be considered simply topics rather than strict theories. But the very fluidity of theoretical boundaries allows the researcher or theorist to wander eclectically across the borders of different schools of thought, which most other theories do not so easily permit. The concepts of structure and change perspectives, however, are relatively simple to understand, which is a reason to introduce them early in this volume. We can thus proceed through the chapters of this book more or less from the simple to the complex, from the less to the more precisely stated perspectives.

Another crucial reason to introduce these perspectives early in the text (although out of the chronological order of the history of social psychology) is that they provide us with a natural introduction to one of the two key questions which we shall raise for each of the sixteen theories of this volume. We have already in Part I considered the first question: How can each theory be used to help the individual person achieve self-actualization? Here in Part II we will raise the other most basic and crucial question: *How can this theory be used to help change another person?* The question is not meant in any Machiavellian sense, but rather as a device to gain insights into human relationships. Indeed, as long as those participating with us in our society, group, or experiment agree in principle to the goals and methods of our attempted social change, then no one can validly claim a moral or ethical foul. The question could be restated as: How can this theory help explain social or personal change? But this phraseology is less concrete, and too often leads to an academic debate or conceptual elaboration. Hence, the question is more directly stated in the prior form above. The readings of Cartwright and Schein (noted for Chapter 3) focus precisely on this question of how to change a person. Of course, if we know how to change another, in most cases we will better know how to change ourselves. Still, the direction of change is left open to our own free choice.

The humanistic-developmental theories of Part I were concerned primarily with the individual person and his psychological progress through life. The theories of Part II focus primarily on *social* and *interpersonal* relations, which gives them a true sociological flavor. This is the case even though the practitioners or social scientists who employ these perspectives in their studies are probably more likely to be psychologists. This anomaly is due simply to the partially random historical development within the two disciplines. Of the authors whose papers are recommended here, only Goode is primarily a sociologist by training. With this historical paradox, it is clear that the boundary lines between the disciplines are quite vague.

Chapter 3

Group Dynamics

Scholarly interest in small social groups brings together a conglomeration of perspectives with many fruitful if disparate hypotheses. **Group dynamics** is in many ways more of a topic and a traditional methodological approach rather than a cohesive theory. Nevertheless, in order to help point to some possible theoretical syntheses of strands we believe it is useful to look at three critical aspects of this and related approaches, namely, primary groups, reference groups, and group dynamics itself. We will content ourselves here with some basic definitions and hypotheses, leaving a fuller understanding to outside reading and classroom or laboratory exercises in small group discussions.

A **primary group** is a naturally occurring group to which one belongs—small, intimate, lasting, and influential on one's basic values in many areas of life. It is also a face-to-face, informal group with diffuse socio-emotional influences based on identification with the members. A **reference group** (or reference relationship) usually refers to a group with which one identifies in his imagination and from which he learns certain norms of behavior, rather than one which he simply uses to compare his ideas. It is not necessarily, as well as not usually, a group of which one is a member, and its influence on one's values can be either positive or negative, leading one to either accept or reject its norms. Lest we forget, we will note the defining characteristics of a real **group,** per se:

1. It comprises a number of individuals who interact with one another on the basis of established patterns.

2. The persons who interact define themselves as group members.

3.   These persons are defined by others as members of the group.

Group dynamics is a rather eclectic tradition of research on laboratory or change-oriented small groups. Researchers typically focus on the main variables which influence the decision or outcome, such as decision-making authority patterns (e.g., democratic, laissez-faire or authoritarian), style of leadership, patterns of communication, group cohesiveness, source and quality of influence, conformity, and how to change people. Typical hypotheses relating such variables include the following: *A cohesive group tends to maintain high conformity among the members. In a cohesive group, attempted influence patterns will be directed at the deviant member.*

Group dynamics research in the observation room is typically aided by tape recorders, one-way windows, and confederates in league with the social scientist. Although the results of such research have been most interesting, there has always been the problem of generalizing from the laboratory to real-life situations. The human subjects in the laboratory are almost inevitably a **secondary group** (role-specific in behavior, oriented to a specific task) rather than a primary group (such as a family or intimate friendship group). Furthermore, such laboratory groups can only with difficulty be considered a reference group, since they are typically of such a short duration that they can have only limited influence on the norms and values of the individual member. A feel for group dynamics is best gained in classroom demonstrations, in practice rather than in theory.

Examples

■   Group dynamics is uniquely suited to changing people. Its principles have been used for everything from psychotherapy to brainwashing in concentration camps to changing delinquents and criminals. Its approach and techniques have been developed or imported into sensitivity groups and management training as well as simulation games for classroom learning. The "good boy" in the "bad neighborhood" has been explained by his self-concept and identification with his nondelinquent primary and/or reference groups, his law-abiding family, best friend, or fictional heroes of good moral stature. ■

This perspective is presented here somewhat ahead of and out of its context of historical development since it grew out of the Gestalt and Field theory and often borrows ideas from the succeeding groups of behaviorist (Part III) and congruency theories (Part IV). The reason for doing so is its orientation towards answering the question of how to change people. This key question is raised in the Evaluation and Application sections after each succeeding theory followed by tentative answers in terms of the basic hypotheses of each theory. This is in one form or another the basic question any theory must answer (as already noted).

See *Recommended Reading and Study Questions* in Appendix, beginning on page 147.

Chapter 4

Role Bargaining

A **role** is a pattern of behavior associated with a position in a society, group, or relationship. These patterns can take many forms. But every pattern of behavior reflects a *culture*, the *personality* of the actor, and occurs in a particular kind of *situation*. Each of these three action systems must be considered for a complete description of a type of behavior. Adapting from a theoretical sociologist, R. L. Warren (1949), a **cultural role** is a "fairly well-defined interaction pattern prescribed by the culture." Such would be the set of expectations common to such classifications of people as husband, student, businessman, or officeholder. A **personal role** is the "personal adjustment to these role patterns," i.e., the peculiar yet regularized way of carrying out the patterns distinctive of a particular individual, referring to such particulars as whether an individual typically enacts his role with vigor (a sanguine role type), with methodical plodding (a melancholic), or with businesslike dispatch (a choleric). A **situational role** is a "short-term interaction pattern worked out within a single, specific situation," such as the tendency for some individuals to dominate or lead, rather than follow in any group of individuals with whom they come into contact.

Within and between such types of role there normally and frequently occurs difficulty of fulfilling role demands known as **role strain** (according to the theoretical sociologist W. J. Goode). In order to come to terms with the strain imposed on an individual (or type of individual) by his various roles, he makes **role bargains.** The flow and eventual routinization of such role bargains develops into a career, a type of behavior, either normal or deviant in character.

After one simply and properly labels the conflicting roles involved, this perspective is one of the simplest and easiest to apply to real-life situations. Furthermore, a thoughtful listing of variables included under the three above-named types of roles can be used as an accounting scheme for describing various types of behavior patterns. Under cultural roles, for example, we could list the following observable patterns: father, mother, son, daughter, businessman, agitator in a social movement, radical student, social reformer, hippie, white-collar criminal, professional thief, heroin addict, chairman of a meeting, servant, dynamic political leader.

Role bargaining is especially useful in sorting out data from case studies of known typical career patterns, such as types of crime, juvenile delinquency, or even for the likes of artists, creative scientists, or self-actualizing persons. In one summary hypothesis, the essence of the theory states: *In the face of conflict between any two or more roles, the individual strikes a bargain with the alternatives in order to resolve the conflict.*

Examples

■   Cultural role factors include one's position in his family (parent, husband, second of three children, etc.), social class, ethnic group, sex role, and occupation, as well as relationship with friends, cliques, etc. Personal role factors include clusters of expectations based on such items as the person's attitudes, self-concept, his relationship to his role model. Situational role factors include expectations related to such things as a person's neighborhood, his transactions in groups of which he is a member, patterns of behavior frequented by persons in his general circumstances, his stage of personal development, the labels his significant others give to him, his pattern of definitions of the relevant situations, and his normal style of bargaining with the options open to him.

A larger example of a case of role bargaining can be seen in the celebrated trial of Sacco and Vanzetti. They were immigrants (cultural role) from Italy to America earlier in this century. Falsely accused of murder (situational role), they were imprisoned. Their sympathy and contact with an anarchist movement (personal role) cast an unfortunate light on their trial. A powerful politician promised to intercede in their court investigation if they promised to renounce the anarchist movement. Their role as persons of freedom and integrity (personal role) was thus in direct conflict with their (situational) role of defendants of their innocency in the murder trial. They staunchly refused to compromise their integrity by refusing to capitulate to the expedient move of the politician. Their role bargain resolved the conflict for their souls but not their bodies. They became symbols of freedom of the human person against authoritarian rule and scapegoating. They also thus became martyrs for the cause because they lost the trial—and their lives. ■

We have deliberately chosen to focus on role bargaining rather than role theory, as the term is commonly used. The latter is a topic or largely descriptive classification system rather than a formal theory. But role bargaining is an explanatory set of statements or hypotheses that makes good and theoretically cogent use of the role concept. It is important to focus in this way on theory in the stricter sense of the word in order to develop the explanatory capability of a conceptual tradition. A conceptual tradition is one that uses descriptive concepts, but which is not yet a theory in the strict sense of the word as defined in the introductory chapter.

See *Recommended Reading and Study Questions* in Appendix, beginning on page 150.

Chapter 5

Interparty Conflict

Although there is much talk of a theory of conflict among social scientists, there is little work that approaches a set of deductively interrelated hypotheses, which, of course, is our definition of the essence of an explanatory theory. We are left then with a wide array of those who sometimes call themselves conflict theorists—namely, dialecticists, Marxists, anti-Marxists, interactionists and anti-structural-functionalists. Because of the confusion, our treatment will be considered unique or even eccentric by many. In order to simplify, it seems desirable to hark back to Georg Simmel for the beginnings of a general theory of conflict. Simmel noted that conflict between parties has positive functions, because it clears the air and creates understanding and even integration between potential enemies. Conflict is more intense when the relationship between parties is closer, when the group is smaller, and when there is an ideological base to the opposition. **Conflict** is defined here in the most general possible sense of opposition of any kind between two or more persons or parties.

The nature of the positive functions of **interparty conflict** needs to be specified, perhaps by looking at the various kinds of goals of interaction such as productivity, smoothness of coordination of joint actions or depth of sharing. Most importantly, it seems that positive consequences come about more surely when the parties have a certain empathic knowledge of one another, and where there is an attempt to bargain with one another fairly. Ideally, the bargaining should be done in an *integrative* manner, so that the joint payoff is greater than the sum of the individual payoffs could be. There will, of course, be differences in forms and outcomes of conflict depending on whether one is looking at a dyad or a whole society. Indeed, there is much work to be done before a theory of conflict can be developed. But the centrality of the concept to the basic task of social science is apparent. From one point of view this basic task is to explain how joint action is possible at all. More pointedly: *How is joint action carried on and developed in the face of conflict between persons or parties?*

Conflict, of course, is not restricted to two parties. In fact, third parties make any situation more complex. Simmel discussed at least four types of triads which have many implications for a study of conflict. A **mediator** is an objective person to whom two persons in conflict present their case, presumably to bring them together. An **arbitrator** is a third party who has some power to resolve differences between the two, from whom they seek support. A **tertius gaudens** leads the other two to vie for his favor and enjoys the fruits of their conflict. A **divide et impera** is a situation where the third party keeps the other two in conflict to dominate them for his own ends.

Examples

■ A simple example of conflict which has positive functions would be a dispute between husband and wife about the family budget. If each party is spending money within reasonable limits of the budget, the conflict is resolvable, in principle. It is only a matter of clarifying their agreed-upon rules for spending. But such a conflict may only be symptomatic of a lack of communication or a problem of mutual affection shown to one another. In any case, to resolve the conflict the couple must gain relevant empathic knowledge of one another's sentiments on the issue. They also need to bargain integratively with one another to develop a monetary policy. Even more importantly, they must try to solve the problem together, for the good of the relationship as a whole. Narrowing their focus on the immediate monetary concerns where there exists a deeper basis for the conflict will inevitably only avoid a resolution or even deepen the conflict itself. The popular advice columns in many newspapers (such as Ann Landers and Dear Abby) are filled with situations of this kind, where the immediate conflict is mainly symptomatic.

Some aspects of the interparty conflict perspective help to explain the confrontation tactics of some members of the women's liberation movement. Political, legal, and verbal attacks on male chauvinism, job discrimination, and abortion laws have had a significant effect on raising the consciousness of men and women both in and out of the movement. One negative effect of this has been to alienate some unbelieving men and women. The tactic consists of creating conflict in the minds of those uncommitted to the movement. Informative facts (bits of knowledge) are usually presented at the same

time as the attack, together with offers or invitations to become a
follower or sympathizer with the goals of the movement **(integrative
bargaining)**. According to the earlier stated key hypothesis for this
perspective, this combination of variables should have positive
functions; in this case, a spread of the movement and more genuinely
equal rights for women. ■

See *Recommended Reading and Study Questions* in Appendix,
beginning on page 152.

Critique of Structure
and Change Theories

REVIEW AND COMPARISON

Here the reader should review the introductions to each of three preceding perspectives of Part II, Chapters 3, 4, and 5, on group dynamics, role bargaining, and interparty conflict. The eclecticism of these theories presents no immediate systematic way of synthesizing them. We must content ourselves with an intuitive overview.

Certain basic concepts from these three perspectives can be nicely intertwined and woven together. Everyone is intimately acquainted with the family and peer group as **primary groups.** Primary groups are also inevitably **reference groups,** though not the reverse. The small social gathering in a **group dynamics** laboratory is however typically composed of **role players** who do not identify very strongly with the other members. The result is that such groups do not have the *influence* over their members or potential members as would a natural small group which is also a primary group or at least a reference group for the person. Usually a person in a unnatural (or laboratory) group will not have any deep purpose in following the group leader. Nor will he intellectually *conform* to group norms except to give the impression he thinks is tactful or desired by the researcher. Deutsch, however, (in the recommended reading) makes a good case for the possibility of generalizing from contrived experiments to real and pressing problems of personal well being and world peace.

Milgram (in the reading) goes as far as to extend some insights from the behavior of animals crowded into small enclosures to the aggressive behavior of men in crowded cities. The almost inevitable problems of crowding suggest that here is a basis for **conflict** that has no easy solution. It is not enough merely to understand the problem in order to solve it. There are limits to the adaptability of the human species. The effort toward accommodation, or integration of persons in social conflict must be accompanied not only by knowledge of the situation, but by a widespread and effective popular desire to resolve the conflict. On a large scale, especially in complex organizations such as offices, factories, or cities as a whole, appropriate channels must be opened up for city planning. Planning for effective use of land and natural and economic resources is done in almost all large cities today. But in too many large cities the urban problems are in advanced stages.

Rehabilitation is necessary. Training for and the availability of jobs is a very central planning factor. However, it is a serious sin of omission to do all this without attention to the needs of persons, of men of all ages and ways of life for a sense of community. Professional spectator sports can, and do, provide millions of people with some sense of symbolic identification with a regional grouping. Television and radio are the chief media to this end. Yet there will never be any substitute for deeper face-to-face contact with one's fellows, especially when there is a common goal of working toward a better world as seen by each of the members. This appears to us as not only an ideal, but as a necessity for the survival of the species, as well as a stepping stone to the fulfillment of every human as a social being. This is the proper end of society and the proper direction of all attempts to change humanity. We need to work together to solve human problems and conflicts. We need to broaden our perspectives so that we can empathize with and more fully appreciate and enjoy the variety of human types, including both the conformist and the peace-loving radical. Clearly, conflict is the most crucial problem of social theory (as discussed in the introductory chapter). Surely this will often be inconvenient, and in the beginning create **role strain** for us. But the sacrifice will be small if everyone participates. Hopefully, then, the **role bargaining** patterns of more and more people of different values will converge upon the Omega point of deeper, more open, personal, and meaningful relations between individuals, subcultures, governments, nations, and civilizations. For without this universal hope the future of mankind is more war. With it, there may be peace.

Evaluation and Application of Group Dynamics

The group dynamics perspective is easy to apply, due in part to the lack of systematic integration and resultant fluidity in the use of its concepts. Only parts of it help much to predict. It has generally moderate information value, and moderate explanatory power. A great deal of research has been done following this perspective, but again it is diffuse and not well integrated.

To change a person, change his primary group or at least his reference groups. Or engage him in a group which he can identify with as a positive, normative, reference group. That group should preferably be devoted to the goals or behavior which you want the person to attain or engage in.

Example

■ Concretely, to change a delinquent who has been influenced by bad companions, it might be a good idea to move him to a better neighborhood. But if his parents are not law-abiding, such a move will help very little. On the other hand, if he is sent to a reform school or boys' ranch where he can meet new boys and learn from them new techniques and forms of delinquency, the delinquency will obviously get worse. The message here for counseling, rehabilitation, and parole or probation officers is simple but profound. Those people who try to help know it too well. Prisoners who are released from jail without new skills will most often go back to their old familiar neighborhood where they naturally slip back into their old circle of buddies, with the expected result of repeated offenses and run-ins with the law. ■

To achieve self-actualization with group dynamics, the person must identify with or join groups which not only have the goal, but in which the members have at least achieved a degree of self-actualization. The problem is to find such a group or collective, and then to become a member. After that, the quality of one's interaction in the group will hopefully help one to achieve self-actualization. Much in the way of social betterment and the quality of relationships between people is closely related to our individual achievement of self-actualization.

Example

■ The group gives support to individual needs and weakness. A sports club with team spirit, and a cheering audience can motivate a lazy athlete. A meditation society, religious discussion group, or prayer circle supports a spiritual need. An encounter group may help a person express his emotions and feelings toward others, which in turn may give him the confidence, satisfaction, and self-esteem prerequisite to achieving his own separate self-actualization. And if the group has a noble goal as its reason for being, say helping the poor, or working toward world peace, then its members are just that much closer to social actualization. ■

Evaluation and Application of
Role Bargaining

The role bargaining perspective takes a somewhat ad hoc and inductive approach to research and theory building, though it leaves open the possibility of incorporating other approaches within its metatheoretical compass. It can be taken as a classification scheme useful for organizing the relationships between the other concepts and perspectives. Yet, it certainly is a highly explanatory theory in its own right. It is one of the easiest to apply because it is so open-ended. This is so at least after the observer has identified the major roles being enacted in the situation under consideration. For the same reason it does little to help us predict, unless we fill in the areas or circles representing the three (or more) basic domains with rich concepts. Such secondary concepts may or may not contain information value in themselves. In itself, the unadorned perspective is lacking in systematically descriptive concepts. This is not to say that the separate traditional topic of role theory does not have innumerable possible classificatory adjectives (Biddle and Thomas, *Role Theory*: 1966). Perhaps because of the same lack of specificity, the explanatory power of role bargaining is dependent upon the background information brought from the concrete case. Since it uses the basic explanatory mechanism of congruency (especially as will be seen in the cognitive dissonance perspective in Chapter 9), it does in a general way help to explain certain basic types of social action or interpersonal change. Unfortunately, research using this perspective is slim and not explicitly related to the perspective because, at this point in its historical development, it is basically descriptive in nature.

To change a person with role bargaining, we must change the cultural, situational, and personal roles which the person has the option to play. We must somehow affect the way roles are taken, situations sized up, and the methods used in bargaining to achieve an accommodation to his options. The manner of achieving this is left quite open. The perspective, per se, gives us little direction until we ourselves can specify the contents of the domains or role types.

Example

■ Heroin addiction has frequently been explained by the "double failure" hypothesis (A. Cohen or Cloward and Ohlin). Most often addicts come from a poor neighborhood where the rate of crime is high to begin with. Since their lower-class circumstances stack the cards of life opportunity against them they are very frequently unable in the first place to achieve the normal success goals of modern society (money, property, possessions, etc.). For lack of contact with organized criminal gangs they seek group support by trying to join a conflict gang, a group of peers who engage in random acts of violence, or "kicks" behavior. They become "double failures" by being blackballed or simply excluded from membership in such delinquent cliques. Or, if the opportunity does arise to commit such acts with a group of acquaintances they may be psychologically inhibited or unable to engage in violent acts or random illegal "kicks" behavior against other persons or property. The result is that they try to find their "kicks" in hard drug use, most often leading to heroin addiction. Their cultural role as a lower-class member is reinforced by the situational role of being excluded from more outgoing peer group relations. Their personal role fits the pattern by manifesting a lack of self-reliance. It is a natural outcome of the role bargaining process when these factors converge on this very problematic delinquent type. ∎

   To change or rehabilitate such a person, role bargaining points to the need for long-term peer group support of a stable nature, together with sympathetic relations with imitable role models. Variations of group therapy have been known to help clients to deal with their situational role difficulties as well as to bolster their self-reliance (the latter being a personal role problem). The Synanon program of milieu-management has probably been the most successful therapy program for ex-addicts. Of course, the existence of such treatment programs gives us no reason to quit working to change the original lower-class family and neighborhood situation which helped to spawn the heroin addict.

   To achieve actualization, role bargaining directs us to make the effort to change our situational environment and background cultural values in order to bring them into line with the personal role we see as most fulfilling in the long run.

Example

   ∎ At a slightly younger age, say in his midteens, the potential heroin user may have had a chance to graduate from high school and go on to college. But in the typical case his reference groups (parents, friends, teachers, peers) do not or are unable to give him much encouragement in this direction. Nevertheless, they still subtly hold up to him such goals as a white-collar job as the only kind of really acceptable occupation. Yet he may by inclination and opportunity be directed into a skilled trade such as that of machinist or carpenter. Blue-collar labor has a second-class status in most of American society, so our potential addict sees his future normal career possibilities as second- or third-rate. Is it any wonder that alienation is so common among workers without a trade or special skill? And it is only a step beyond such unpromising expectations to drug addiction for our victim of slum-ghetto living.

There are expectations, though. The "good boy in the bad area" is one who somehow manages to carve out a respectable place for himself with the help of a good, stable family life (cultural role) and application to school work stimulated by a teacher who either "hits it off" or who takes special pains to establish rapport with him (situational role). A "good," i.e., nondelinquent self-concept (personal role) is the key to containment of possible delinquency. Even if he does not make it to college, he is likely to have a positive career image of the blue-collar worker to give him motivation to study, to learn a trade and live a self-actualized life (personal role) within the restricted circumstances of his life chances. ■

Evaluation and Application of Interparty Conflict

The interparty conflict perspective, insofar as it has been pulled together as a distinct perspective, seems to have been developed on an inductive base, but its more recent use has been as material for deductive elaboration. It is easy to apply because of its open-endedness. When it does apply, it helps to predict moderately well. It has moderate information value, and moderate explanatory power. Empirical support is more intuitive than objective. It is rarely explicit due to the generality and diffuseness of its propositions.

To change a person with interparty conflict, engage him in a process of empathizing and (distributive or preferably integrative) bargaining or constructive conflict in order to lead him to act as you would prefer. According to our suggested basic hypothesis for this perspective, the goal of such conflict will hopefully be the promotion of deeper relationships between the parties, or greater productivity as a result of their joint efforts.

Example

■ Two nations at war, or who have a basic conflict of interest, ought to make efforts to solve the problem. A long-standing case in point is the Arab-Israeli conflict which has lasted over the past quarter century (from 1947 into the 1980s). Mutual empathy was severely limited by a lack of peace talks and negotiations of any kind (either integrative or distributive). Without such there could realistically be no peace, let alone joint productivity, nor even a positive relationship of any kind. With negotiations, especially if they can be brought to the integrative stage (say of mutual free trade), there could finally develop sincere friendship between the neighboring nations. ■

To achieve self-actualization with interparty conflict we should engage in constructive conflict, presumably to resolve our differences, as well as to set boundaries around our actions based on more exact knowledge of the opposition party's interests and values. This might suggest the need for opening ourselves up to others, taking the risks of deeper involvement, which also inevitably means the risk of greater conflict. (The reader can easily draw other implications for achieving actualization from the hypotheses of Simmel.)

Continuing the previous illustration, circles of mutual interest could be developed between the Arabs and Israeli among common cultural, and perhaps religious, grounds. Maslow's need ladder shows how the need for love and affection, or here for positive relationships with one's neighbors, must precede the attainment of self-actualization. Nations at war can hardly achieve a sense of fulfillment, especially since both sides inevitably lose much in war. And the joy of triumph gained at the expense of one's neighbor is only a mixed and temporary high for a person or nation with solid moral principles.

Sample Comparative Write-Up

A Theater Play Analyzed with
Group Dynamics and Actualization
Angel Street, a play by Patrick Hamilton (1939), will be used to illustrate the perspectives of group dynamics and actualization. The story is about Mrs. Bella Manningham. Her husband, Mr. Jack Manningham, is a villain who tries to torture her into madness. She is accused of little thefts and deceptions. The insinuation is made that she is insane just as her mother was. He even uses one of the servants as a shill to reproach her until she is half-convinced that she is indeed mad. In actuality, he is the maniacal murderer who fifteen years earlier, in the same house, killed a rich old woman but failed to steal her jewels because he could not find them. He is still looking for them. His motive for torturing his wife is to gain time to continue looking for the jewels. Through it all Mrs. Manningham still trusts him and is the obedient wife. She is happy at going to the theater with him, and

enjoys serving tea and muffins. A benign police inspector helps her to unravel the plot.

As background material, the *theoretical* problem here is that of the type of accommodation style that may result from pressures devastating her self-concept. The *practical* problem is: How can she cope with the threat to her self-concept? Time 1 will be defined as the original circumstances in which she finds herself before she suspects the plot on the part of her husband. Time 2 is the resolution period, after she finds out. The crucial intervening event or turning point is the visit and aid of the old police inspector.

Group Dynamics Applied to Angel Street

For Mrs. Manningham the police become an important reference group, especially when she discovers the plot of her husband with the help of the benevolent police inspector. Concerning the types of reference group, she is obviously not a member of the police force. But they are for her *normative* and *positive*. She holds the norms of the police (rather than simply comparing herself with them). They are a positive reference group for her, but a negative reference group for her husband. Until she discovers the plot, her husband forms a positive reference relationship with her. Furthermore, she and her husband form a primary group. They are in fact a nuclear family, as well as a small, intimate, diffuse, face-to-face, actual group or relationship which influences the members to conform to the norms of the other(s). Some characteristic group dynamics hypotheses would indicate that we look more closely at the process of decision-making within the relationship and the apparently authoritarian basis for interaction between them. Because of the tight cohesiveness of the marital relationship, group dynamics would lead us to understand why she almost conforms to his insinuations, why he almost convinces her that she is, in fact, insane.

Actualization Applied to Angel Street

The reader should here review the summary introduction to Chapter 2 on social actualization, noting especially the five steps of Maslow's need ladder. Mrs. Manningham does manage to satisfy the survival needs of step one, the need for food, clothing, shelter. Her needs at the second step for physical security and safety were probably satisfied from her point of view, although she finds out later, when her husband's dire plot is discovered, that she had been all along in potential danger of losing her life. At step three, her needs for love and affection are met only with small occasional tokens of affection on the part of her conniving husband. The older maidservant (Elizabeth) was really the only one in the beginning who showed any real concern for her. As the plot develops, the old police inspector shows genuine concern for her welfare when he steps in to discover and reveal the plot against her.

At the fourth step of the need ladder, Mrs. Manningham has a very low self-regard and severe self-doubt as a result of her confined circumstances and her husband's continual attempt to undermine her confidence. It is clear that she could hardly expect to have this since her prior needs for love and affection were continually denied and underfulfilled. Under such circumstances she could never expect to achieve step five, self-actualization. It is not until she finally sees through her husband's plot that she gains a strong measure of self-regard. She then confronts her husband in a subtle way so as to show her ultimate mastery over him. At this moment, although the fruits of a kind of revenge on her part are somewhat negative in tone, she does express her newfound freedom from bondage and ignorance in a peak experience that indicates a kind of self-actualization.

Evaluation and Application of Group Dynamics and Actualization

Table 1 is presented to aid the comparison. Although the ratings are subjective, the device is very helpful to most students. Group dynamics is not difficult to apply, but it requires the imputation of certain missing elements in order to apply it fully. For the present example, the idea of a relationship rather than a group as such must be used. Initially it was unclear exactly which terms of the perspective applied in the first place, since the story is primarily concerned with only two persons whose other relationships do not form a group at all, but only separate relationships. Actualization is rather easy to apply because of the simplicity of the five steps in the need ladder. The story gives sufficient depth of character study, and covers a moderately long period of the life history of the main actors. Of course the satisfaction of Mrs. Manningham's needs beyond the first two or three steps is only very minimal.

The information value of the group dynamics perspective is low because the terms apply to short-term, small decision-making groups rather than to this relatively long-term natural setting. The idea of group loyalty, however, does provide some information. Beyond the

TABLE 1.1

	Group Dynamics	Actualization
Ease of Application	4	4
Information Value	2	3
Predictability	2	3
Explanatory Power	2	3
TOTAL	10	13

notions of group pressure and influence toward conformity, the information provided by the perspective is little. The information value of actualization is only moderate, since it gives us little basis for describing the subtleties of her self-doubt and only a vague idea of her confinement and mental torture. The theory gives little information about how one advances from one step to another. It does not tell us about the process of *how* her lack of self-regard was contingent on receiving love and affection. It tells us only that there is such a contingency.

The numerical ratings are based on the reasons given in the preceding text. A rating of "5" is high, "1" is low. If you are willing to give equal weight to each of the four criteria, at least for practical purposes, it is possible to sum up the ratings for each theory. The theory receiving the highest number might be called the best theory. At very least, it is most interesting and provocative in discussion to raise such questions in the classroom periodically throughout the term, naturally with an ever increasing repertoire of theories to compare. It should not be necessary to say that any such quantitative rating is only tentative. And it certainly applies only relative to the other theory used, and for the particular example analyzed. A theory may receive a very low rating as a formal theory and still be highly provocative for any given analysis. It is far too early in the game of social theorizing to close off good ideas, no matter how loosely stated.

The predictability of the group dynamics perspective as a whole, especially as treated here for the beginning student, is relatively low because it consists mainly of concepts without an explicit synthesis of hypotheses. Without some synthesis of hypotheses based on some central explanatory principle, prediction is bound to be chancy, at best. The perspective would tend to predict that Mrs. Manningham would conform to her husband's insinuations in the lack of support from other people, e.g., the servant or the police. It certainly does not predict at what point she will believe the police rather than her husband. Actualization must receive only a moderate rating on predictability. It does permit us after some degree of juggling of concepts to predict that she will not achieve self actualization until she achieves some measure of self-regard. And this is in turn dependent on fulfilling to a certain degree her need for love and affection. We do not receive any help from the theory itself however in predicting the specific nature of her needs. We must read this into the circumstances of the drama.

The explanatory power of the group dynamics perspective as applied is low. It explains to some extent why she did as her husband wanted early in the action, through the notion of primary group loyalty. It does not explain why he did his deed, and little reason is given for why the police inspector took an interest. The explanatory power of actualization is only moderate, at best. It tells us in general *why* Mrs. Manningham could not achieve the higher steps of the need ladder. Again, we must read into the story the exact nature of the prohibiting factors. It does at least help us to explain why her self-esteem increased when she discovered the plot. The self-esteem was only in a sense and indirectly based on the inspector's "love" for her welfare as a human being. In fact, her self-esteem was dependent more on the discovery of the plot itself, rather than on the "love" or altruism granted by the inspector.

At this point the students should begin preparing a simulation game. See Appendix, beginning on page 171.

Part III

BEHAVIORISTIC THEORIES

The following three behavioristic theories have taken hold more among psychologists than sociologists. Exchange theory is nevertheless applicable to sociological problems as well. As we shall see, game theory can also be applied to whole nations, especially if we conceive of the nations as embodied in their diplomats over the bargaining table. In any case, both of the latter two perspectives have developed naturally out of S-R, the stimulus-response behaviorist model of man as a black box. Man is a mysterious creature who does strange and wonderful things. We can observe what goes into the box (inputs), the person (or group). And we can observe what comes out (outputs). We may call these environmental or experimental preconditions **inputs** and the behavioral results of the person's adaptation or coping as **outputs.** Here we have a kind of computer model of man. We must look only at his observable actions, or behavior, in effect largely ignoring for the moment his thought processes, self-concept, and his possibilities for long-range planning.

There has undoubtedly been more hard, quantitative research done under the banner of these theories than with any other group of theories. And this is their hallmark. Modern empirical psychology has developed from the behaviorist model which originated just after the turn of the century. The convenience of the laboratory has produced an immense literature which mainly reports research on extremely specific and rather narrowly focused hypotheses.

From this point on in the text, the remaining groupings of theories proceed in a historically chronological order of development. Although there is a vast amount of overlap, we can certainly say that the period in which the strictly behavioristic theories (Part III) originally flourished preceded that of congruency theories (Part IV), which in turn largely preceded the contemporary flourishing of social interaction theories (Part V). It is chancy to estimate which grouping is dominant today, but as a rough approximation it would be generally agreed that variations of stimulus-response behaviorism are still dominant among academic psychologists. And certain varieties of symbolic interactionism (and perhaps exchange theory) are predominant among social psychologically oriented sociologists. There is a fair amount of crossing over disciplinary lines among individual researchers, but nothing yet approaching a general rapprochement.

Looking backward to Part I, the actualization perspective was developed largely by renegade psychologists revolting against the behaviorists. And identity development (Erikson's neo-Freudian approach) is used primarily by the nonbehavioristically oriented clinical or counseling psychologists. The counseling approach is individual and analytical, rather than directed toward verification of hypotheses with quantitative observational data. Naturally, it is still wide open to debate and discussion as to which approach is more useful and productive. There are, for example, huge numbers of clinical psychologists who use a behavioristic approach and huge numbers who use some variant of psychoanalysis as therapy. The student must judge for himself which theory best fits his needs. And in what circumstances does it fail to fit?

Chapter 6

Stimulus-Response Behaviorism

A long and venerable tradition of primarily laboratory research, **stimulus-response behaviorism,** began in earnest with the work of John Watson after the beginning of this century. The perspective in one of its early formulations indicates in part that hedonism ("Pleasure stamps in, pain stamps out," as per Thorndike) is the primary motivating force for animal and human behavior. In other words, we behave or respond to the stimuli that comes into our path. Although many sophisticated researchers (like Clark Hull) have elaborated on the basic hypotheses to make them more inclusive of the complexity of human behavior, S-R generally is more applicable to the behavior of lower animals. There are two basic forms of behaviorism: classical and operant conditioning.

Classical Conditioning

Presentation of a sequence of events in the laboratory (or in any closed system) produces certain basic reactions in the subject animals. Thus, 1) an unconditioned stimulus (UCS) (such as meat presented to a dog) leads to an unconditioned response (UCR) (the dog salivates). 2) The same unconditioned simulus is then presented in conjunction with a conditioned stimulus (CS) (such as the ringing of a bell), which again produces the same unconditioned response (namely, saliva in the dog's mouth). 3) The unconditioned stimulus is eliminated. Only the conditioned stimulus is now presented (to the dog), which still produces the conditioned response (the saliva in the dog's mouth). This is a classical example of **classical conditioning.**

Operant Conditioning

Operant (or instrumental, or reward) **conditioning** works on *responses* or behavior which has *already occurred*. The researcher may reward this behavior in order to stamp it in, which is known as **approach** (or enticement) conditioning. Or he may punish undesirable habits (i.e., give a negative reward) in order to stamp it out, which is **avoidance** conditioning. A rat may receive a reward of food for completing a maze (approach conditioning), or the rat may be relieved of electric shock in his cage by pressing a bar (avoidance conditioning).

Both types of conditioning are incomplete in themselves. Certain key concepts must be added to these sequences of hypotheses before social behavior can begin to be explained—namely, imitation and secondary reinforcement. **Imitation** occurs in behavioristic types of patterns. One kind of imitation is **matched dependence** in which followers must depend upon the leader for the cues as to what act is to be performed and where and when. The other kind of imitation is **copying,** in which the imitator attempts to produce responses which are an acceptable reproduction of the behavior of the model person, without inducement. Both types of imitation are said to occur because the individual is rewarded for imitation (according to the leading psychological researchers, Dollard and Miller: 1941).

The other concept (besides imitation) which must be brought in to more easily explain social behavior is that of **secondary reinforcement,** which is simply a second reward associated in the mind of the subject with the primary one. If I feel satisfaction walking on the beach in the sunset, I receive my primary reward. But if I walk on the beach in the sunset with my girl friend, her presence may then become my secondary reward or reinforcement associated in my later thought and feeling patterns regarding the beach at sunset. The precise interrelation between these concepts is left vague by the behaviorists, as are the conditions of reinforcement and the interplay of more complex cognitive processes.

In order to more easily address the key theoretical problem of this text, we need to take a look at S-R's five general ways to change behavior. Bandura and Walters describe the following ways:

    1. **Extinction,** which involves a decrease of response strength due to removal of reinforcement, which leads the animal to become frustrated and, in turn, no longer to respond to the stimuli presented.

    2. **Counterconditioning,** which is eliciting incompatible responses by presenting negative along with the positive rewards, such that there is no longer any reason to emit the previously expected response.

3. **Positive reinforcement,** which is the essence of the approach type of operant conditioning, i.e., the use of rewards to increase the strength of a response tendency.

4. **Social imitation,** which was briefly discussed above.

5. **Discrimination learning,** in which the occasions and stimuli for making a given response are distinguished within the animal based on patterns or schedules of reinforcement.

These terms are basically variations on the important notion of schedules of reinforcement (except for imitation). The notion is so important that no less a figure than B. F. Skinner has devoted his career to elaborating upon the idea with research and theorizing.

Examples

■ The principles of S-R apply to learning any basic skill, or as a foundation for therapy to overcome behavioral pathologies. Applications have been made to help the physically handicapped to gradually develop their limited skills through a well-planned and gradual rise in successful accomplishment and expectations, known as a **schedule of reinforcement.** The emphasis is on the rate and number of occurrences of a given behavior as a result of controlled variables. The same principles can help a person learn to walk, learn a language, drive a car, or play baseball. Bad habits, such as drug abuse, alcoholism, bed-wetting or bad table manners, can be broken. S-R has even been used to develop teaching machines, to train armies, and to sell cars, deodorant, and toothpaste with sexual association and enticement. ■

See *Recommended Reading and Study Questions* in Appendix, beginning on page 154.

Chapter 7

Exchange Theory

The essence of **exchange theory** is the equation borrowed from economics: *Profit = Reward − Cost*. Therefore, a person will seek out and persevere in those activities and relationships which provide him with the greatest profit. Profit must be considered from the person's own point of view (not the view of the observer/scientist), as the person himself defines the situation. Of course, the rewards and costs incurred depend upon the subjective values and relative satisfactions of the person under study. Relative profit for a person also depends on what he sees as his best opportunities and least acceptable outcomes (as pointed out by the group psychologists Thibaut and Kelley: 1959, through their terms **comparison level** and **comparison level for alternatives**). In related work, George Homans is the eminent sociologist most associated with exchange theory. He focuses on comparison of rewards and costs by emphasizing the concept of *distributive justice,* or what the concerned persons consider fair for the exchange situation under consideration. Homans (in dealing with exchange theory) has also discussed the rewards and costs in terms of the activities, interactions, and sentiments of the parties, and how these result in **norms** and behavior patterns (the key concepts of his five comparative case studies analyzed in his classic work *The Human Group,* 1950).

Exchange is very easy to apply to an exceptionally wide range of life situations. It may well be the most popular perspective in social science today. Insightful and predictive, it must be used with the chief caution that the scientist not impose his own value judgments on the persons under study. Though many social scientists would disagree, it is our opinion that the best and only truly valid research can be done by taking as primary the definitions, perceptions, and values of the people being studied. These may need interpretation by the observer, but they are primary.

Examples

■   Applications are almost unlimited. Wherever there is conversation between two people, exchange theory can be put to use. Any interactions with reciprocal giving and receiving are possibilities, whether the exchange be of presents, words, ideas, or mere glances. A student may gain useful knowledge from talking to his teacher (a reward gained at little cost). In turn, the teacher may gain satisfaction at being helpful, or receive praise and gratitude for his efforts (a reward gained at little cost but his time).   ■

See *Recommended Reading and Study Questions* in Appendix, which can be found on page 156.

Chapter 8

Game Theory

Game theory is an application of mathematical thinking to gamelike situations, namely, to situations characterized by two parties making choices which have interdependent outcomes or payoffs. This perspective is basically an extension of exchange theory to situations of mutual interdependence. Thus, a **payoff** is the profit or loss resulting from the gamelike exchange of costs for rewards. The theory requires thinking that is a little more precise than usual because of the difficulties of sizing up and quantifying possible outcomes of the parties. But the effort is well worth the result in terms of ideas and hypotheses generated.

The quantitative matrix (usually with four cells) of payoffs is essential. Figure 8.1 is a simple example. Here, A represents one party to the transaction, B the other. The payoffs of A are listed first in each of the four cells, those of B second, according to the notation (A, B). Both A and B have two choices.

Example

■ Two sons must decide what to do with a family business after the parents have died. If both want to sell it and divide the proceeds, then each will receive 3 units of money (e.g., $30,000 each), represented in the diagram by (+3, +3). If both decide to work together and improve the business they could sell it in a couple of years and make more, although the cost in time and effort would be greater. We can represent this by (+4, +4) in the matrix. If the elder brother, A, wants to sell and the younger, B, does not, an arrangement will have to be made so that B can buy A's share in order to continue the business on his own. At the moment, the matrix shows that A and B still come out equal (+3, +3). However, if A wants to save the business and B does not, B would receive the same payoff (+3). But it could well be that the older brother, A, could quickly increase the value of his share with his savings and greater business experience to a +4, giving a matrix of (+4, +3).

If the two brothers see the situation fully, then we can predict that A and B will both want to keep the property because this has the possibility of highest payoff for each. B will always want A to keep it so that he, B, has the one possibility of gaining the +4 payoff. A will be indifferent to what B does since A has control over the outcome. If A

FIGURE 8.1

A

		Keep	Sell
B	Keep	+4, +4	+3, +3
	Sell	+4, +3	+3, +3

(A, B)

keeps, A gains 4. If A sells, A gains 3. If B keeps, A can cause B to gain either 4 (if A keeps) or 3 (if A chooses to sell). If B sells, B gains 3 no matter what A does. If B keeps, he still gains at least 3, but can gain 4 if A keeps. ■

See *Recommended Reading and Study Questions* in Appendix, which can be found on page 157.

Critique of
Behavioristic Theories

REVIEW AND COMPARISON

The reader is reminded here to review at least the introductions to the separate chapters 6, 7, and 8 (on S-R behaviorism, exchange and game theories) of Part III. It should be observed that the central behavioristic notions of individual **behavior** and **reinforcement** are the basis for the development of **social exchange** theory. The elaboration is complicated by the consideration of two or more persons simultaneously responding to one another in observable ways. **Game** theory went a step further, beyond the $Profit = Reward - Cost$ equation. Mutually interdependent moves and outcomes or profits must be considered as a matter of course with this perspective. Exchange and game theories are social by definition. S-R itself may be individual or social depending on the application.

In the introduction to Part III, we noted briefly the relations of the behavioristic to the humanistic-developmental theories. Among those structural and change theories of Part II, it is true that **group dynamics** (Chapter 3) has close ties to the behavioristic approach. It deals primarily with small laboratory groups and most often the researcher collects hard, quantitative data to test carefully and even operationally stated hypotheses. Yet the grandfather of group dynamics, Kurt Lewin, favored a **field theory** approach which encompassed a wide range of data and variables in effect from both sociology and psychology. His followers were a heterogeneous breed. Many of them became involved in small-group laboratory research, while a significant number moved toward a more direct and applied approach, either toward industrial psychology or toward the humanistic movement.

Role bargaining (Chapter 4), as another of the structure and change theories (Part II), is clearly an extension and elaboration of exchange (a behavioristic theory). However, the elaboration was in the direction of more typically sociological questions, such as the interpersonal, family problems, relationships between social classes, and even to the alleged battle between the sexes.

Conflict theory (as treated in Chapter 5, Part II) in itself is a more typically social or sociological approach (although the suggested readings were written by psychologists, Deutsch and Milgram). It was suggested that Georg Simmel (a philosopher claimed as a founder by sociologists) was one of the original thinkers in the early development of ideas about interpersonal conflict. But conflict theory has also developed immensely in recent years from another sociological direction, that of Marxism, which seems more useful for reviewing broad historical developments based on class conflict. Whether it is possible to integrate the micro (of Simmel) with the macro (of Marx) remains for future scholars and imaginative students to decide. Behaviorism in itself does not seem to prohibit a marriage with the dialectical. In any event, exchange and game theories have often been used to study questions of conflict between two or more parties. In fact, these two could be easily placed in the family of conflict theories.

The humanistic-developmental theories (Part I) are definitely concerned with conflict, though they typically lean more towards ideas of resolution of conflict inside the person rather than towards conflict between parties. It again becomes clear (as discussed in the Introduction) that conflict is the most central concept and problem demanding explanation by social theory. Such a statement implies the strong possibility that any explanation for the conflict, or its causes, processes, and outcomes will also contain within it a theory of how social order is possible in the first place. Practically and tactically speaking, however, the more useful question to ask still seems to be how social order is possible in the face of conflict.

Evaluation and Application of Stimulus-Response Behaviorism

The perspective of S-R behaviorism was developed as a methodological strategy to encourage researchers to operate inductively. But in practice much research done in this tradition works from the simple assumptions deduced from the S-R model, no matter how simplistic they might be at times. It is very easy to apply S-R to controlled laboratory settings, but it must be stretched to realistically apply it to natural settings or real on-going group interaction. For the ordinary observer, it provides little in the way of descriptive information or concepts (although some sophisticated formulations like those of Clark Hull and even B. F. Skinner are notable exceptions). It helps to predict only in highly controlled or laboratory settings. In such narrow circumstances it has high explanatory power. But again, in complicated natural settings, group interaction, novel situations, or those involving the self-concept and reflection, S-R quickly finds its limitations. Still, more research data has been gathered in this tradition than in any other.

To change a person, Walker and Heynes (1967: p. 98) tell us how to condition him by using S-R principles:

> If one wishes to produce conformity for good or evil, the formula is clear. Manage to arouse a need or needs that are important to the individual or to the group. Offer a goal which is appropriate to the need or needs. Make sure that conformity is instrumental to the achievement of the goal and that the goal is as large and as certain as possible. Apply the goal or reward at every opportunity. Try to prevent the object of your efforts from obtaining an uncontrolled education. Choose a setting that is ambiguous. Do everything possible to see that the individual has little or no confidence in his own position. Do everything possible to make the norm which you set appear highly valued and attractive. Set it at a level not too far initially from the starting position of the individual or the group and move it gradually toward the behavior you wish to produce. Be absolutely certain you know what you want and that you are willing to pay an enormous price in human quality, for whether the individual or the group is aware of it or not, the result will be CONFORMITY.

Example

■ A case of how to change a person can be seen in the clever real estate salesperson dealing with unskilled house hunters. The salesperson begins by showing the buyers a charming house which will cost more than they want to pay. One assumption is that the buyers could really afford to pay more than they are presently willing. Here the goal is offered which is "appropriate to the need," a charming and cozy home. This would fulfill an "important need for the individual." The element of "conformity" in this case is paying the extra money, which is "instrumental to the achievement of the goal" of owning the cozy dwelling. The buyers can be "prevented . . .

from obtaining an uncontrolled education" by trying to bring them to an early decision and not telling them all the possibilities for the failure of their investment. The early decision will not allow the buyers much time to visit other realtors. And the normal agreement among salespeople is that once a buyer has been shown that particular house by that particular salesperson no other salesperson will have the right to consummate the sale to that buyer. The "setting . . . is ambiguous" because of the huge number of houses for sale as well as the fact that the buyer is a novice in home buying. He will also for the same reason have "little . . . confidence in his own position." The good salesperson will take special pains to point out all the advantages of the neighborhood, convenience, and niceties of this house for this customer. That is, the salesperson will "do everything possible to make the norm which has been set appear highly valued and attractive." The norm will be set "at a level not too far initially from the starting position of the individual . . . and move it gradually toward the behavior the salesperson wishes to produce." It will be done by first showing the buyers a house for sale at their originally desired price, which will almost surely not be as nice as the "dream house" which the salesperson wants them to buy. Finally, if all these conditions are met, and the buyers are eager to find a house, they will quite likely buy the "dream house." "The result will be CONFORMITY" to the wishes of the salesperson. ∎

To achieve self-actualization with S-R principles, we should continually hold the carrot of the next step in our life plan firmly before our mind's eye until we attain fulfillment or are well on the road to attaining it. We should set a long-range goal and decide as accurately as possible what intermediate plateaus we must reach and can reach.

Example

∎ If I decide that my self-actualization will be best achieved by devoting my life to the service of others, say in a medical profession, I will inquire about and enroll in a program of studies in a medical school and work part-time in a related job to test my interest. Each year I will review my plans and reflectively take account of my deeper feelings and needs. If my overall feelings of genuine satisfaction in the service of others' medical needs grows each year, then I can be rather certain that in my lifetime career choice I am on a truly self-actualizing path. ∎

Evaluation and Application of
Exchange Theory

The exchange perspective takes the deductive approach, attempting to apply the basic equation $(P = R - C)$ to all concrete interaction situations. For most applications for most students, this is probably the easiest of any perspective to apply to a large number of situations. It is in effect universally applicable, which contributes to its outstanding explanatory power. In situations with a limited number of variables it has moderate information value and high predictive potential. Empirical support is mounting for the exchange perspective due to its fashionability in recent years.

To change a person, we must manipulate or modify their values (= perceived rewards) so that what is perceived as rewarding is what we want them to do. We must also attempt to lessen the cost they perceive it will take to do it.

Example

■ A teacher can try to point out the intrinsic rewards of learning a subject for its own sake, or out of a pure desire to learn, or for practical applicability to the student's future career. This will increase the student's motivation, thus increasing the amount of reward aimed for. The student's costs will be lessened if it is felt that the assigned study is meaningful rather than mere "busy-work." With such low costs and high reward, the value of the course of study will be high relative to most courses, and the student will be motivated to change—by studying harder for that course. ■

To achieve self-actualization with exchange theory, we must arrange our priorities so that our rewards, in the short, and above all in the long run, will be actualizing for us. Alternative life styles other than those which are truly actualizing must be perceived by us as having higher costs. A systematic procedure for setting up this kind of personal reward system is that of "Program Development" among specialists (like R. Carkhuff) in the area of human relations development.

Example

■ A career of hard drug use may have its momentary highs, but if prolonged without sound medical reasons it will inevitably take its toll on physical and emotional health. The user will become a victim of his deviant career choices, thus producing higher long-run costs for him than a more normal career would entail. A young person's interest in drugs could well be channeled in the direction of a challenging career which would more likely be self-actualizing in a natural way, such as that of a chemist, pharmacist, biologist, doctor or nurse, or perhaps even drug rehabilitation counselor. This would provide more lasting, meaningful contact with persons able to fulfill his need for love and affection, which should give him self-esteem, and prepare the way for occasional excursions into the natural highs and peak experiences that do not depend on drugs. The reward will almost always be more rewarding to the person in the long run. The costs of immediate self-denial of drug indulgence depend on the person and his situation and values. Highs can, of course, be reached with drugs, but they are hardly a basis for long-run fulfillment. ■

Evaluation and Application of Game Theory

The games perspective uses an explicitly deductive model, although the payoff matrices could easily be developed inductively. This perspective is more difficult than most for the beginner to apply, especially for the student who is unaccustomed to quantifying social variables or carefully analyzing two-party decisions. However, once it is applied, it normally has very high predictability, moderately high information value, and very high explanatory power. A great deal of research data has been gathered using the games perspective, but almost exclusively in closed laboratory settings. We believe it has great potential, however, for at least ad hoc application to natural, everyday settings, not to mention such global applications as the arena of international relations.

To change a person we would engage him in a relatively closed, game-like situation. Then we would arrange the payoffs so that we have behavior control over him and his choices, and choose our alternatives accordingly.

Example

■ If I want to change a person I must manipulate the situation or wait until the opportunity arises whereby his choices are all dependent on mine. It is even easier if I can obtain my goal in changing him with either of my options. Say, for example, the only two sons must dispose of a family business after the death of the parents (as in the illustration

FIGURE A

Fate Control

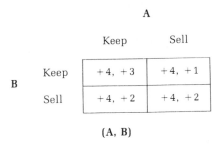

(A, B)

opening Chapter 8). If the matrix of perceived payoffs fails in a certain way, then A can have fate control over B's payoffs. Such is the case in Figure A where we see that the circumstances are such that no matter what choices are made, the older brother, A, will receive a payoff of + 4. But if B chooses to keep the property (in a partnership), in hopes of gaining the + 3 payoff, A can exercise fate control over B. Thus, if A chooses to sell, B gains only + 1; if A chooses to keep, B gains his maximum possible outcome of + 3.

To achieve self-actualization with game theory, we should somehow arrange to have our long-run payoff turn out in an actualizing way. This will very likely come about in non-zero sum games in which the joint payoff for cooperation is greater than that for distributive or zero-sum situations. ■

Example

■ Figure B is an appropriate matrix for a relationship between two nations in conflict. They can each either hold out or cooperate with one another. If either or both holds out, their payoffs are equal and opposite, i.e., what one wins the other loses. These are known as **zero-sum** situations, because their total scores always sum up to zero. But on the other hand, if both nations A and B decide to cooperate with one another, they can gain a separate payoff of + 5, which is higher than either could gain separately. And their total payoff is then + 10, which is a total of ten units more than either nation could gain without mutual cooperation (if the total for both is considered). This could be brought about by pooling of natural resources, for example. The result in the latter cooperative case is much more likely to be social actualization, as well as individual actualization. ■

FIGURE B

Trust and Suspicion

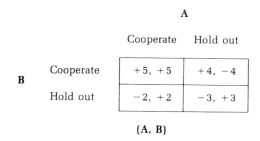

(A, B)

Part IV

CONGRUENCY THEORIES

This set of four perspectives is psychologically oriented at root, since each focuses on an individual person, or on an individual in an interpersonal relationship or setting. The four are cognitive dissonance, symmetry, interpersonal congruence and self-consistency. Each deals with some psychological or social conflict from the point of view of the single person with a problem. All except self-consistency were developed in the laboratory or quasi-laboratory setting. All four depend on the basic assumption that *an individual who senses conflict within himself will inevitably try to resolve it*. The source of conflict may be based on conflict with another person or group, and may be only secondarily sensed inside the person. However, the natural or normal drive towards conflict resolution or congruency is characteristic of each of these four perspectives. In this same sense we can see that the congruency perspectives make definite assumptions at least about this one basic internal drive in the person. This is the kind of assumption that the strict behaviorists are typically unwilling to make. (Some behaviorists do however posit a different assumption, that of a mechanism leading a child to imitate a parent, as we have seen in Chapter 6.) The congruency drive seems a natural one to lay down, though perhaps somewhat limited in its ability to explain the extreme variety of human types and cultural values of people in far-flung lands throughout the world. Yet laboratory researchers, and Lecky as a counselor, have found it an extremely productive principle for their separate purposes.

This congruency principle in effect broadens somewhat the methodological principle of the behaviorists that we should only, or almost exclusively concern ourselves with overt, directly observable behavior. This is so in that a mental mechanism is brought in as a central principle. Conceptually, these four perspectives are exceptionally simple. With a little thought we can easily see countless applications and illustrations of the truth of the congruency principle.

Chapter 9

Cognitive Dissonance

Cognitive dissonance, a perspective developed by Leon Festinger in the psychological tradition, is very open-ended and easily applicable to a wide variety of life situations. It is based on the common experience that *a person who has two or more dissonant ideas in his mind will try to reduce the sense of dissonance and achieve consonance among the ideas.* He will also tend to avoid situations and information which would increase the dissonance. Dissonance usually occurs after one makes a decision with some commitment that strongly affects subsequent behavior. It may arise from logical inconsistency, conflicting cultural mores, past vs. present experience, or a case where a specific nonfitting opinion is included in a general opinion. In short, **dissonance** is the awareness of contradictory ideas. Its strength depends on the importance and number of dissonant elements in one's mind in relation to the importance and number of consonant ideas.

Example

■ A common instance of dissonance is the person who smokes two packs of cigarettes a day when he realizes that smoking causes lung cancer. Many other illustrations could be given. Confrontation tactics, as used in existentialist psychotherapy, aim at creating dissonance to raise the self-awareness in the patient of his illogical and inconsistent behavior and thought patterns. Once his irrational defenses are broken down in a therapeutic atmosphere, he can be guided to change his ways. Confrontation tactics as used by peace marchers, radical students, or even by some airline hijackers, are frequently aimed at creating awareness of a bad social situation in the minds of the general public or administrators and government officials, who would otherwise ignore such social evils. The Boston Tea Party at the start of the American Revolution was aimed at creating cognitive dissonance in the minds of British rulers over the fact that American colonists paid tax without being represented in the British government. ∎

As a further qualification, there are three basic ways of reducing dissonance: 1) to change the discrepant behavior (e.g., to stop smoking); 2) to change the environment or seek support (e.g., to associate more with fellow smokers); and 3) to add new cognitive elements (such as telling oneself that smoking is relaxing).

Dissonance is said to be more in evidence when one passes some turning point in life or just after a crucial decision. However, there are exceptions to the attempt to reduce dissonance. These are likely to occur when the usefulness of the new experience or information outweighs the threat of dissonance. In such a case, dissonance-arousing experience and information will be sought out.

Let us sum up some of the defects and exceptions to the rule of avoiding cognitive dissonance:

1. The bare definition of the perspective does not consider the degree of inconsistency of the discrepant ideas.

2. It inadequately specifies the conditions of different forms of dissonance.

3. There is an unsatisfactory conceptualization of the type of motivation involved in the pressure for dissonance reduction.

4. Lastly, paradise is seen as a lack of tension (Deutsch and Krauss, 1965: 69–70).

Finally, dissonance is tolerated under the following conditions:

1. The attitude object, or the issue at hand, is relatively unimportant, or at least less important to the actor than other relevant values or interests.

2. The pertinent social relationship (between actor and other) is unimportant, at least on this issue.

3. The issue is confused, but perceived as having the possibility of being sorted out by reflection.

4. Or, the subject or actor feels it is crucial to his long-range goals or values to discover inconsistencies or dissonance-producing bits of knowledge now or in the short-range.

See Recommended Reading and Study Questions in Appendix, beginning on page 159.

Chapter 10

Symmetry

Theodore Newcomb's social psychological perspective on attitude change and interpersonal attraction focuses on **symmetry** in interpersonal communication. It is easily summarized in a diagram (Figure 10.1).

A is usually the **person** or actor of primary interest, the one whose behavior or ideas are open to change in the situation under consideration. B is the **other** person (party or group) in the relationship. X is the **attitude object,** the thing, norm, third party, idea, value, or whatever is at issue in the present circumstances. The arrows between A and B indicate their **attraction** to one another. The arrows from A or B directed toward X indicate the **attitude** of A or B toward that attitude object. A + (plus) sign indicates a positive attraction or attitude. A − (minus) indicates a negative attitude or repulsion in the direction indicated by the arrowhead. These attitudes and attractions also vary in intensity (which might be indicated in various ways, such

FIGURE 10.1

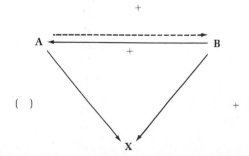

as by a double plus sign, $++$, or a double minus sign, $--$, or a '0', for highly positive, highly negative, or neutral, respectively).

Symmetry exists between two persons when three conditions are met: signs of attraction (between A and B) are alike (either both positive, or both negative); when signs of attitude (A to X, and B to X) are alike (i.e., both positive or both negative); and intensities (of attitude and attraction are respectively) equal. Thus in the diagram, we would be able to predict that over time, A would become negative in his attitude to X. The presumption is that where symmetry does not exist, the parties will communicate with one another or otherwise change their intensity of attitude or attraction; or in general, change their behavior or ideas until such symmetry is gained, or regained. This perspective thus has essentially the same defects as cognitive dissonance. And of course, if the relationship is shallow or the issue is unimportant to the two parties, then the theory does not apply.

Example

■ To illustrate, if A and B are both mutually and equally attracted to one another, and A has a positive attitude toward X, then we would predict that at some later point in time B would gain a similar positive attitude toward X. More concretely, if A and B are husband and wife respectively, and A (the husband) likes chicken soup, but the wife initially does not like chicken soup, then we would predict that over time she (B) would eventually learn to like chicken soup (X). Other typical applications involve acquaintanceship, roommating, friendship, mating and marriage, or family life. All kinds of informal social groups and relations between nations could also easily be analyzed with symmetry. ■

Elaboration of these ideas, and more complex diagrams could easily be drawn to illustrate the attitudes of a pair toward several attitude objects simultaneously, and through several periods of time. It usually is simplest to use a separate $AB - X$ diagram for each period of time and each attitude object separately. What this procedure provides us is a handy way of describing attitudes as affected by interpersonal relationships, feelings, perceptions, and influences.

See *Recommended Reading and Study Questions* in Appendix, beginning on page 160.

Chapter 11

Interpersonal Congruence

A sociologist, Backman, and a psychologist, Secord, combined efforts to develop an interdisciplinary middle-range theory of a more formal variety, useful especially for interpreting surveys and laboratory research on dyads or small groups. Their approach (as stated in their original theoretical article) is at points quite technical and detailed. But the main ideas of **interpersonal congruence** can be rather simply stated with some slight reinterpretation of the original, as follows: There is a threefold matrix composed of the subject's **concept of himself,** more or less as a total picture (symbolized by SS); the subject's **behavior** with regard to the present issue and situation, *as he himself views it* (Sb); and the subject's **perception of the behavior of an other party,** which has some bearing on the issue at hand (SOS). In using this matrix, it usually is easiest to focus on a single issue at a time, even though many issues may be involved between the two parties to the problematic situation. On any given issue, these three components may or may not be congruent with one another. All three may be incongruent with one another. Or one of the three may be incongruent with the other two.

One possibility is that element 1, the subject's self-concept may be consistent with element 2, his behavior on the issue at hand, but element 3, his perception of others' behavior towards him on this issue may be out of whack. He will then presumably try to make the matrix congruent by trying to change the others' behavior towards him on that issue. He will then have changed the one incongruent component to match the other two. He might also have tried to change the two components to match the one (i.e., to change his self-concept and his behavior on the particular issue in order to achieve congruence with his perception of the others' behavior toward him on that issue). Or he could modify all three components to achieve a completely new congruent matrix.

Example

■ Figure 11.1 gives a matrix which will help us to analyze the case of a citizen signing a petition, and the nature of the petition. The columns represent the three elements of the matrix; the rows, the times before, and after the event. The crucial event here is the signing of the petition. Time 1 is before he signs, and time 2 after. Element 1, his self-concept (SS) as a whole is only strengthened by the event of his signing the petition for something he believes in. Close to the core of his self-concept, he sees himself as a believer in democracy. By the signing he feels he has exercised his right and duty as a citizen in a democratic country. Let us say that the petition was directed at the legalization of the Communist party. As a believer in the democratic idea of free exchange of ideas, he feels that membership in any party should be allowed so long as they do not plot and foment to overthrow the government by force or violence. In short, at time 2 his self-concept of himself as a truly democratic citizen is reinforced by this event.

FIGURE 11.1

	1) **SS**	2) **Sb**	3) **SOS**
time$_1$	Democratic	Upright citizen	S feels others see him as an upright citizen
	C	C	C
E= event	S signs petition permitting membership in Communist party.		
time$_2$	More fully democratic than ever	He sees his behavior on this issue as fully consistent with the constitution of his democratic fatherland	S knows that some others now see him as undemocratic or revolutionary and a threat to their way of life
	C	C	I

His behavior on this particular issue, element 2 (Sb), is that of an upright citizen. He behaves in a way fully consistent with the constitution of his democratic fatherland. Thus, his behavior at time 2 does not change, and he would sign a petition like this if the occasion arose again. Element 3 (SOS) however, is somewhat problematic. He sees at time 1 that others view him as an upright citizen. However, after he signs the petition he realizes that some of his acquaintances now see him as undemocratic or revolutionary, and perhaps even a threat to their way of life. At time 1 all three elements were congruent with one another. Now at time 2, element 3 is somewhat **incongruent** with the other two (indicated by the "I" in the lower right box). Depending on the strength of his perceived conflict with his acquaintances on this issue, he may modify his position either by organizing against communism, or perhaps by joining a group devoted to the active promotion of civil liberties. Notice that the C's in the three boxes of the time 1 row indicate congruency. The single "I" in the time 2 row indicates matrix incongruency.

One advantage of this perspective is the fact that it forces the researcher or theorist to explicitly treat the three key concepts, which involve both the pertinent psychological as well as social factors on an issue, in a specific interpersonal situation. Because it is so specific and explicit, however, the perspective of interpersonal congruence may not be as applicable to such a wide variety of situations as some other more vague theories. Such careful statement is nevertheless the very crucial element lacking in most other social psychological theories. ■

See *Recommended Reading and Study Questions* in Appendix, beginning on page 161.

Chapter 12

Self-Consistency

Self-consistency is a unique perspective developed by Prescott Lecky, a scholar and teacher with practical experience as a counselor. In agreement with many other theories of the human social personality, he found that people are basically motivated by the need to maintain a consistent set of images about themselves. And when basic inconsistencies are pointed out to them they will go to great lengths to correct the discrepant self-images. The precise mechanisms by which they do this is left unstated, but probably follows the general pattern of the cognitive dissonance approach. The central hypothesis of **self-consistency** is: *Given significant inconsistencies in ideas about themselves, people will try to deal with them by either changing their behavior or their ideas to achieve congruence.*

Lecky's use of configurations of a person's self-concept is a deceptively simple way to develop a relatively complete and accurate picture of a person in a short interview. As an aid to such description, he suggests the listing of personality traits, key images and life experiences by arraying them in three concentric circles. The center circle contains that person's ultimate life concern, as far as can be discerned, which represents the **core** of his self-concept. Listed around the second or **middle** circle would be major life interests, values and experiences. And on the **outer** circle would be listed the more peripheral, but still somewhat influential background items and patterns of activities, all concisely phrased in a word or two.

Example

■ If a configuration were developed for a person with a problem or conflict of ideas about himself, the inconsistencies could then more easily be pointed out to him in a theoretically valid context. This counseling device would hopefully motivate him to try to resolve the discrepancy. If, for example, a high-school student (see Figure 12.1) were having difficulty with mathematics but wanted to become an engineer, especially if he were not fully aware of his own problem, the use of such a self-consistency configuration would then be helpful. It might be a help in allowing him to see that he either must lower his aspirations or do better in mathematics, perhaps with special help or simply a more determined effort. ■

See *Recommended Reading and Study Questions* in Appendix, beginning on page 163.

The two italicized items are inconsistent. The remaining factors will have a definite influence on his attempt to resolve the problem. The actual attempts to change the pattern will have to be worked out in practice.

FIGURE 12.1

High-School Student at time 1

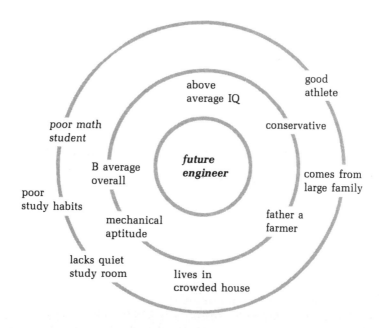

Critique of
Congruency Theories

REVIEW AND COMPARISON

The **congruency** principle is so useful that it has been borrowed by theories even outside of this fourth grouping. It is the principle of motivation for change, at least implicitly, in role bargaining (Part II, Chapter 4). Indeed, role bargaining as treated above is very much of an extension and elaboration of congruency into the social realm. This is of course a point in favor of role bargaining, though the same fact should cause us to beware of oversimplified application of any perspective. As noted in the exceptions to cognitive dissonance, we must be alert to the qualifications of the congruency principle which would lead us inadvertently to overlook the frequent human search for incongruency and rebellion, as well as the human failure at times to seek the deeper and more long-range goals.

The reader should review the summary introductions to the perspectives of Part IV, in Chapters 9, 10, 11 and 12 (on cognitive dissonance, symmetry, interpersonal congruence and self-consistency). Within this set of perspectives we can see that **cognitive dissonance** is most basic. Because of its openness and generality, it is the starting point for development of the other perspectives. **Symmetry** builds on cognitive dissonance by bringing in a second person, a specific attitude object, and a communication process. **Interpersonal congruence** is more specific in the use of its three basic conceptual elements. **Self-consistency** focuses on a configuration of images around a conflict within the self.

The idea of the self reminds us of the perspectives treating of self-actualization (Chapter 1), self-identity (Chapter 2), and personal role (of role bargaining, Chapter 4). The idea of self foreshadows for us (and was, in fact, developed largely out of) the tradition of symbolic interactionism which follows next (in Chapter 12).

The utility of the congruency principle is too great to underplay its value. But it is also easy to overestimate its true value unless we who employ it take care, as any good researcher would, to make a case for the rival hypothesis of a search for incongruity. Finally, social research is hardly worthy of the name unless it takes account of other persons, groups, relationships, the social context, and the actor's definition of the situation. This term again foreshadows the symbolic interactionist perspective.

Evaluation and Application of Cognitive Dissonance

The cognitive dissonance perspective is basically quite uncompli-cated. It is founded on a single deductive premise, which was likely at one time developed intuitively by some common-sense enquirer into the motives of human action. The reader will, of course, recall the premise that if a person has two ideas in conflict he will try to resolve them by changing his ideas or behavior. As a perspective, cognitive dissonance is one of the most universally applicable and hence, easiest to apply to concrete cases. It helps us to predict that some change may come about under given circumstances, but it does little to tell us what will happen. It is not very informative when it comes to telling us whether ideas or behavior will change, or in what direction they might change. However, in cases where it does fit, it explains, at least after the fact, the basic reason why a certain change does occur. There is a vast amount of related empirical support for the perspective, including some field and survey applications, but still largely done in laboratory settings by Festinger and his followers.

Using the principles of this perspective, a person could be changed by somehow creating undesirable dissonance for him in all situations except the one in which he does what you want him to do. Do it regularly and consistently, perhaps with occasional variations. The problem however, is to know what will cause those dissonant ideas to arise in another person's mind. Those ideas may change and/or depend on the situation, which may well be unpredictable.

Example

■ A person who is a heavy smoker could create dissonance for himself by fining himself 50¢ for each cigarette he smokes, and donate the proceeds to the cancer research fund. He could be reminded by the mass media that statistics show that the average life span of a smoker is decreased by the length of time it takes him to smoke a cigarette. For every ten minutes of cigarette smoking he will lose ten minutes off his life. The person who wants to stop smoking could seek support by joining a group aimed at helping people to stop smoking. Or, he could also ask friends to remind him to desist when he habitually begins to smoke without considering the consequences for his health. ■

A person could at least make beginning attempts to put himself in situations which his experience has shown lead him to peak experiences, or tastes of a sense of self-actualization. Cognitive dissonance could be created to remind one of less valuable situations, situations which seem to be less likely to produce ultimate self-actualization. This, of course, requires enough self-knowledge and experimentation with different life-styles or rules in order to know what works for you. Dissonance might be easier to create around undesirable or nonpeak experiences. Naturally, actualizing experiences cannot always (or even a large part of the time) be directly aimed for and rationally attained. Thus, the utility of cognitive dissonance here is somewhat limited.

Example

■ It would be possible to create mild cognitive dissonance for oneself or others when situations arise which experience has told us will prohibit self-actualization. Thus, a parent, teacher, or friend may occasionally and tactfully remind us of our tendencies toward compulsive buying, excess in the use of food, drink, tobacco, drugs, overwork. These reminders are occasions of purposeful cognitive dissonance. These may help us to prepare the way for later religious or contemplative experiences which can then become an integral part of our fulfillment as a person. ■

Evaluation and Application of Symmetry

The symmetry perspective is at root a deductive type of hypothesis or perspective in that its central principle is rarely modified by new data. Naturally, qualifications are made for particular types of situations based on new data. But the central principle remains. It is exceptionally easy to apply when the elements of the case to be analyzed involve two persons interacting over some attitude object. In uncomplicated circumstances, it helps to predict change in behavior or attitude or communication patterns, but the direction of that change remains unpredictable. Hence, it helps to describe a given case in a limited sort of way. Its explanatory power is also somewhat limited because it applies primarily to situations of attitude change between two persons. However, a rather large body of literature supports this perspective.

To change a person, the symmetry perspective would tell us to become friends with him, and then engage in activity which would lead him to feel as we do on the desired attitude object. Get him involved and communicate with him about it. For example (in Figure A), if I am A, my girl friend is B, and the attitude object X is our potential marriage, clearly we both like one another very much. I want to get married. She is yet uncertain (indicated by the empty parentheses along the arrow flowing from B to X). The way to change her attitude of uncertainty is to communicate about the possibility or perhaps try to persuade her while maintaining, or even increasing our mutual affect for one another. Unless she has powerful alternatives available outside the relationship, we as observers would predict that she will eventually agree to get married.

To achieve self-actualization with symmetry, the perspective directs us to associate with people who are self-actualized, especially with those who are actualized in ways which appear attainable by us as individuals.

Example

■ If I frequently need to relax my nerves, I may seek out a yoga class or a meditation society (represented by party B in Figure A). A is myself. X is the goal of relaxation which both I and the other group members are seeking. Through communicating with them (A-±-B), they will reciprocate (B-±-A) by teaching me proper techniques of meditation. Thus we eventually support one another in our goal of relaxation through meditation. We achieve a measure of separate self-actualization. And as a group we can approach a deeper appreciation for one another, or even a kind of social actualization. ■

FIGURE A

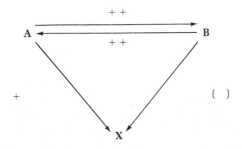

Evaluation and Application of Interpersonal Congruence

The perspective of interpersonal congruence uses a generally deductive approach based on application of the three terms of the configuration. It is more difficult for the average student to apply than most other perspectives because the observer or researcher must be able to fit the three key concepts directly and accurately to the concrete case. If the case requires other concepts than the three, or if the three do not fit well, then the perspective must be abandoned. It applies for this reason to a limited number of cases, perhaps, more so than do most other social psychological perspectives. Yet, when it can be applied, it has high information value because it is more explicit. It predicts somewhat better than cognitive dissonance in most applications, again because it is more explicit. Finally, it is good on explanatory power because it specifies the mechanism or sequence of interpersonal events which give the reason why change or stability occurs in a person in a relationship. Much research has been done employing this perspective in laboratory-type settings, where it applies best. But we should not neglect its potentially insightful application to everyday settings.

To change a person with interpersonal congruence, we must create the social or interpersonal conditions which will influence him to engage in the desired behavior. We might, depending on the circumstances, try to change his self concept, his image of himself on the issue at hand, and/or change his perception of what the relevant other or others think about him on the issue.

Example

■ Figure B gives an outline of the analysis of a changed radical. Time 1 is before, and time 2 after the crucial intervening event. The event is the radical's discovery that extended usage of marijuana causes brain damage. Before the event his self-concept (element 1) was that of a radical, but changed at time 2 to that of a prudent ex-radical. His behavior itself (element 2) at time 1 involves that of smoking pot often. Later, at time 2 he uses pot only rarely. His perceptions of others' views about him (element 3) at time 1 are that his "straight" friends look up to him and consider him "hip" or "in." At time 2, he must put up with the fact that most of his "hip" friends consider him a "straight" or a "cop out." We can see that the threefold matrix at time 1 is congruent. But at time 2 element 3 is somewhat out of joint with elements 1 and 2. We might predict that he will communicate his

FIGURE B

	1) SS = Self = concept	2) Sb = Subject's behavior as he views it	3) SOS = Perception of other's view of him
time$_1$	Radical	Smokes pot often	S feels his straight friends look up to him and consider him "hip" or "in "
	C	C	C
E = Event	Discovers extended use of pot causes brain damage		
time$_2$	Now he becomes a prudent ex-radical	He now uses pot only rarely	S knows most of his "hip" friends consider him a "straight" or a "cop out"
	C	C	I

discovery of the dangers of drug abuse to his "hip" friends, seek new friends, or tolerate their disapproval of his changed or reform behavior. ■

To achieve self-actualization with interpersonal congruence, we would have to first decide what our self-concept as a whole looks like now, in contrast to what it would be like when self-actualized. Then we would have to set about changing it, in part by seeing our specific behavior or actions in the new light of our desired future self-configuration. This would also involve attempts to change others' views of us as persons in order to bring their perceptions into line with our desired self-image and personal being.

Example

■ In Figure C we have a chart of an analysis of a person who joins a group devoted to meditation and social action. This is the crucial event which causes the change from time 1 to time 2. His actual behavior beforehand (element 2, SB) is undisciplined and inconsistent with the possibility of attaining self-actualization. After he joins the group, he gains in personal and social integrity so that he can now

FIGURE C

	1) **SS**	2) **Sb**	3) **SOS**
time$_1$	S recognizes he is not a self actual- izing person	S's behavior is undisciplined and inconsistent with attainment of self-actualization	S seeks feedback from friends about his life style and discovers a selfish streak
	C	C	C
E = event	S joins a meditation and social action group.		
time$_2$	S gains in self-esteen and comes closer and closer to self- actualiza- tion	His new group activity rein- forces his per- sonal and social character integrity so that he now has more frequent peak experiences	His friends, new and old, show concern, i.e., love and affection, thus fulfilling his need at this step at a deeper level
	C	C	C

experience more frequent "peak experiences." Beforehand, when he sought feedback from his friends (element 3, SOS) he began to learn that he had a selfish streak that was inhibiting deeper relations with many people. Afterwards, both his new and old friends show concern for his development as a person; i.e., they express love and affection, thus fulfilling his need at this step of the need ladder. Concerning his self-concept as a whole (element 1, SS), beforehand, he recognizes that he is not a self-actualizing person. This may have motivated him to join the group. Afterwards, he gains in self-esteem and comes closer and closer to self-actualization. At both points in time there was congruency (noted by 3 C's in each row) between the three elements. The change was motivated from inside himself or due to accidental events which led him to join the meditation and action group. At any rate, this is a peculiar case in the application of the perspective in that the change was not motivated by incongruency between the three elements of the perspective. ∎

Evaluation and Application of Self-Consistency

The perspective of self-consistency uses an inductive mode because it begins with counseling observations. It provides only an approach rather than an explicit theory for analyzing change in a person's self-concept. It is very simple to apply because everyone can be described in its terms. And everyone is intimately interested in his own self-concept. It is most informative when a good counselor is using it. It does not help much to predict the future of the person, although a person who consciously used it as an analytical device could predict a certain at least desirable direction of change in his behavior or self-image. As a theory per se, self consistency does not explain very much. But as a tool for counseling it can be most useful in explaining patterns of individual behavior or directions for needed change. There is unfortunately little literature or research done explicitly using this perspective. It could be most fruitfully used by counselors, analysts, and researchers of counseling encounters.

To change a person with self-consistency, we must demonstrate to him certain inconsistencies about himself, which will lead him to change or adapt in the way we see as desirable.

Example

■ A political office seeker may seek to displace the incumbent member of an opposition party which has seen bad times. A famous example is the Watergate affair of political spying by wire-tapping, which put Republican party members and President Nixon in trouble during following elections. In the wake, succeeding Republican office seekers seemed to lose credibility, as well as lose elections. The opposition Democratic party office seekers made this an issue even in the local elections with success. They appealed to the need for political honesty. In effect, this appeal raised a doubt in the minds of many Republican voters, such that their own self-consistency was called into question. Their self-concept as honest people came into contradiction with their membership in the Republican party, or potential vote for a Republican candidate. Thus, this appeal of Democratic candidates resulted in a change in the behavior of voters based upon a sense of their own possible self-inconsistency. ■

To achieve self-actualization with self-consistency, we must become fully cognizant of the blocks, conflicts, and inconsistencies inside ourselves. Then contrast these barriers with a common-sense plan for facilitating the emergence of our better urges and more fulfilling impulses.

Example

■ Many reform and religious groups (e.g., the Catholic Church, and even cell groups of the Chinese Communist party) have used the notion of confession of one's faults or sins as a means to internal reform of the person and the group. The effect is to help purify the person of hindrances to his personal betterment, usefulness to society, and—depending on your point of view, ultimate salvation, or self- and social actualization. Freedom from personal faults, however, is clearly not enough. Positive virtues must be cultivated and personal service rendered to society before actualization can be obtained for self or for society. ■

SAMPLE COMPARATIVE WRITE-UP

Theater Play Analyzed With
Cognitive Dissonance and Role Bargaining

Cognitive Dissonance Applied

The reader should here review the plot summary of the play *Angel Street* in the *Student Use* section after Part II (p 55). The essence of cognitive dissonance, as we have seen, is that a person who has two ideas in conflict will try to resolve that conflict by either changing his ideas or his behavior. Mrs. Manningham had so much mental conflict that she was on the verge of insanity. The two specific ideas in conflict were: 1) her conception of herself as a loving wife, and 2) the deceptions (perpetrated by her husband) which pointed to her apparently mentally unsound behavior. The deceptions were reinforced by the words of the husband and one of the servants. Since Mrs. Manningham was unable to reconcile these two ideas, she moved on occasion in the direction of seriously doubting her own sanity, which was a type of change in her ideas. At the same time her behavior showed more and more seemingly bizarre twists as a result of the continual mental pressure on her from almost all directions. The latter represents a change in her original behavior, from the time before her husband began putting this kind of pressure on her.

Role Bargaining Applied

The essential notion of the role bargaining perspective is that a person who has a conflict between the duties of two or more of his roles will try to resolve that conflict through a process of role bargaining. Mrs. Manningham senses a conflict between 1) her role as sane human being, and 2) her role as loyal, devoted wife, especially when she is cruelly treated by her husband, and still more so when she begins to discover his plot to drive her insane. At this realization she begins to bargain in the only way realistically possible to her, namely with her accustomed role relationship with her husband. She begins however reluctantly to reevaluate the evidence, guided by the police inspector, so that she gradually realizes the truth of his evil intentions. It is difficult for her to accept the discovery and its significance for her past life with him. But after she is able to observe the evidence and accept the facts, her mental sanity is no longer in question, which no doubt provides her with a great catharsis. In any case, she can now realize the bargain to reconcile her personal role as sane person with her new role as woman freed from an evil man and false husband.

Evaluation of Application of
Cognitive Dissonance and Role Bargaining

Table A summarizes the comparison of the four criteria for a good theory. The ease of application of cognitive dissonance is very high. The essential point about Mrs. Manningham's plight is one of her conflicting ideas. Her ideas and behavior are affected to an extreme degree by the mental conflict born by her. Role bargaining is easily applied once we discover the nature of the conflicting roles played by her. After that, the nature and direction of her role bargaining are easy to pick out. Her conflicting roles of sane person, and cruelly treated loyal wife, lead to her struggle of bargaining with these roles.

With this overview we can see that once again in the long run both theories provide a part of the truth. Neither theory is complete by itself.

TABLE A

	Cognitive Dissonance	Role Bargaining
Ease of Application	5	4
Information Value	4	4
Predictability	3	4
Explanatory Power	5	5

The information value of cognitive dissonance is somewhat above average. It helps us to nicely describe the process of change in her way of thinking. It is limited by its concentration on only three concepts. Coincidentally, these concepts are exactly those crucial to an understanding of the present story. The information value of role bargaining is better than average, at least if we follow up the implications of the subordinate, descriptive concepts listed under the three basic types of roles. The cultural role factors would direct us to look at her roles as wife, citizen and mistress of the household. The notion of situational role directs our attention to the isolation of her house in the neighborhood, the limited contact with anyone but the servants and her husband, her role as daughter of a woman who went insane, and in general, her limited contact with anyone outside the household. The personal role factors point to her initial lack of another person of her general social standing and life circumstances to identify with, until the police inspector intervenes. Her subservient attitude and normal self-concept, at least under normal circumstances, are also indicated by her personal role factors. In combination, these subordinate but component role adjectives are very helpful for a truly informative analysis.

The predictability for cognitive dissonance is moderate. We could easily have predicted the recovery of her normal behavior and freedom from serious further self-doubt by reference to this perspective. This is so only after we discovered the intervention of the benign police inspector. Role bargaining here is only a little above average in helping us to predict. With the aid of the theory we know that Mrs. Manningham must either become insane or somehow deal with her treacherous husband, or some combination of the two. We cannot accurately predict ahead of time which alternative will follow. As observers of the play action, we are initially unable to know whether or not she is already partly insane.

The explanatory power of cognitive dissonance for this story is very high. It very economically gives a reason why Mrs. Manningham behaves and thinks as she does, both before and after the discovery of her husband's plot. It is somewhat limited, however, by a lack of specification of why a person will tolerate a high degree of dissonance as she did for such a trying period of time. Role bargaining has a quite high explanatory power because once we pick out the conflicting roles played by Mrs. Manningham we can easily see why she acts as she does. We can see that she does not immediately believe the inspector's story because that would contradict her traditional primary role as loyal, devoted wife. However, she does listen to the inspector because of the threat to her sanity posed by her isolation and her husband's yet unrealized trickery.

Everyday Application: Three-Page Write-Up for Cognitive Dissonance

In order to gain a better feel for the application of cognitive dissonance to everyday encounters, the following assignment is useful.

1. Break a norm.

2. State which norm you broke. The circumstances should be some in which you can readily observe the reactions of others, and in which you will have a moment to analyze your own movement of ideas and behavior.

3. Summarize your norm-breaking experience.

4. Explicitly describe the key points of the cognitive dissonance perspective as applied to your experience. In other words, a) Explicitly stipulate which two ideas were dissonant in your mind. b) State what change or confirmation of behavior occurred in you at the time. Or, state why no change in your behavior occurred, if that is the case. c) State what change or confirmation of ideas occurred in your mind during or just after the norm-breaking incident, if any. d) Predict your future behavior and ideas with reference to the norm you broke.

Remember that to break a norm is not necessarily to break a law. Plan ahead. Ultimate responsibility falls on your shoulders. Ideas such as those used on the "Candid Camera" television show would be ideal for this task.

The student should use the standard format shown on page 31 for writing this report.

Part V

SOCIAL INTERACTION THEORIES

This set of four perspectives is sociological in orientation and relatively recent in origin. It includes symbolic interactionism, labeling, dramaturgy and ethnomethodology. They have been developed and are used largely by those with sociological inclinations. Symbolic interactionism is a metatheoretical frame of reference, in part a kind of philosophy which can easily be used to begin to integrate or incorporate all other social psychological theories within its scope. To attempt such a task in detail, however, is a lifetime's work. The reader should at least prepare himself to observe how certain of symbolic interactionism's central concepts have been elaborated into tributary (or branch) perspectives. For example, the actor's definition of the situation, including his labeling of himself, may be strongly influenced by the labels given to him by the significant other people around him. These others are thus part of his reference group, or may even be members of his primary group (see Chapter 3). In any case, these labels and their effects on the person are the essential concepts of the labeling perspective (Chapter 14).

Dramaturgy (Chapter 15) is a perspective developed essentially around the attempt of persons to put themselves in the shoes of another (i.e., to take his role, and then to behave in a way that manages the impression that the other person receives. The effect is that of setting the stage and even playing discrepant roles (i.e., being in effect two-faced) in order that the second person will define the situation in a way desired by the first. Those who call themselves ethnomethodologists (Chapter 16) can be seen as sort of avant-garde dramaturgists. They basically inquire more deeply into the person's definition of the situation with methods suited to uncover the rules governing the inner workings and nature of the social order occurring in relationships between two or more persons.

The original development of the line of thought represented in this set of social interaction theories was a conviction on the part of certain so-called pragmatist philosophers that the popular stimulus-response behaviorism (S-R theory) school of thought (Chapter 6, Part III) was not suitable for the adequate study of the full range of human social behavior (cf. Mead's *Mind, Self, and Society*). S-R was most suited to pigeons, rats and monkeys, rather than to self-conscious role players, living in complex groups and societies with highly developed and variable social institutions, such as educational, governmental, economic and family systems. Congruency theories (Part IV) can be seen as specific applications and elaborations of aspects of the central interactionist concepts of mind and the social act (see *Critique* of Part V for more detail). Symbolic interactionist concepts have very often been used for theoretical grounding of developments of the social actualization perspective (Chapter 1). Even Erikson's central concept of identity (see Chapter 2) is closely related to the symbolic interactionist notion of the "self-concept," or at least to G. H. Mead's "full development of the self." Still another practical application has been made by the insightful and influential clinical psychoanalyst, Harry S. Sullivan, who was very strongly influenced by Mead's ideas.

We have seen how the structure and change theories (Part II) are fluid and cross-cut many other lines of thought. Role bargaining, for example, is an elaboration of the central symbolic interaction concept of the social act, with its exchange of gestures and role-taking. The reader who has not looked ahead, but has read this book in order of presentation, will not yet be familiar with all the concepts being cited in this introduction (to Part V). But it seems useful to sensitize ourselves ahead of time to the multiple possibilities for a tentative synthesis of most of the theories in this volume. Again, symbolic interactionism seems to hold out this possibility to many students. There can be little doubt that it is the broadest in scope as well as the conceptually most fully developed of all perspectives presented in this volume (with the possible exception of certain interpretations of S-R behaviorism). Still, it has quite a way to go.

Since theories in general are frequently somewhat difficult to understand for most introductory students of social psychology, this more complex one of symbolic interactionism has been placed in the last part of this text. Students with less fear of theory and more preparation than average could profitably read this chapter much earlier. Most students, however, for pedagogical reasons, need some preparation and experience in dealing with theoretical concepts in a systematic way before tackling the refinements and sometimes the necessary vagueness of a broader perspective like symbolic interactionism. In any event, symbolic interactionism can well be viewed as a culmination point and a plateau for the future progress of present-day social psychological research and inquiry.

Chapter 13

Symbolic Interactionism

Home base for understanding **symbolic interactionism** is the **social act**, which is a process of interaction between two people, say A and B (see Figure 13.1). Person A **gestures**, thus indicating by some manual or verbal symbol his intention or plan of action toward person B. B **takes the role** of A, interpreting, or imagining what role A is playing in order thus to gain directions for his own (B's) behavior. Person B then gestures back to A and A in turn engages in role taking in order to decipher or decode B's message. And the cycle proceeds until the conversation or interaction terminates. A set of such social acts, if communication is reasonably successful, should develop a degree of **consensus** between the two parties, facilitating future interaction and the eventual development of elaborate patterns of interaction with a community of persons or a whole society. Meanings, especially social meanings are then deciphered by interpreting behavior over a set of recurring situations.

Role taking, as part of an individual's "definition of the situation" occurs primarily in the mental or reflective processes of an individual, which in themselves are predominantly linguistic. As such, role taking is a factor which distinguishes human beings from lower animals. These reflective processes involve mental images of others and self in context. The **self-images**, or pictures of oneself when looked at as a whole configuration constitute the **self-concept**, the most important and solid part of one's inner processes. These processes involve an internalized conversation of gestures between the "I" or impulse to act; and the "Me," or censuring images which result in what we generally call **self-control**.

Sometimes it is difficult for the beginning student to make a direct application of the social act to a series of events over a period of

FIGURE 13.1

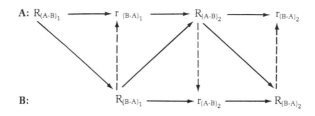

time. Figure 13.1 is a short-hand diagram (Cottrell: 1942) which is very helpful in this regard. The line or row of letters and symbols after the letter A includes the gestures and thoughts of person A. The upper case R's represent A's overt behavior, gestures or responses. The lower case r's represent A's mental pictures or images of the other party's (B's) overt responses (R's). These mental images (lower case r's) are gained through the process of role-taking (indicated by the dotted vertical arrows in either vertical direction). Moving from left to right, across the top line, $R_{(A-B)_1}$ means the original behavior or response of A to B. $r_{(B-A)_1}$ is the mental interpretation by A of B's first response to A, etc. $R_{(A-B)_2}$ is the second overt response of A to B. The dotted arrows moving horizontally from left to right simply indicate the line of direction of A's actions and thoughts. Naturally line B represents the overt and covert behavior of person B, the other party to the conversation or interaction. The heavy arrows moving slant-wise from capital R to capital R indicate the main overt, observable actions of A and B to one another.

Example

■ $R_{(A-B)_1}$ can represent the opening gesture or statement of a wife, A, to her husband, B. She says "Let's go to a movie tonight."

His first response is $R_{(B-A)_1}$: "I'm too tired, dear. I had a hard day at the office."

She takes his role, i.e., mentally interprets his first response to gain the mental image of his feelings, $r_{(B-A)_1}$, thinking to herself that he is really not at all so tired.

Accordingly she responds overtly, $R_{(A-B)_2}$: "You promised last weekend that we would go. Besides, Bergman's latest drama is playing at the Neighborhood Cinema. Our favorite director. And there were rave reviews in Movie Monthly." (This is probably the turning point, or crucial intervening event in the action which leads to a resolution.)

He takes her role the first time he has the opportunity in this sequence, to gain the image of her intentions, $r_{(A-B)_2}$, thinking to himself that he had been wanting to see that film for a month now.

He then responds again, $R_{(B-A)_2}$, by giving in: "OK, we'll go to the 8:30 performance so I can get to sleep early." ■

See *Recommended Reading* and *Study Questions* in Appendix, beginning on page 164.

Chapter 14

Labeling

Labeling, as a perspective in social psychology, has its roots in scattered sociological sources. It is related to the psychological school of Gestalt which deals with a figure-on-a-ground, or contextual perspectives dealing with social perceptions. The researchers in the labeling tradition are dominated by those with a preference for case studies and participant observation. Theoretically, the perspective flows naturally out of the interactionist tradition. Some of its leading figures are Edwin Lemert, Howard Becker, Sykes and Matza, and Thomas Scheff. Labeling seems to best fit the inductive approach to theory building, since it begins with naturalistic observation of concrete cases. Then later the researcher proceeds as would a good ethnographer, from particular observations to general propositions about social behavior in a particular context.

At the risk of premature formalization, the following nine-step explanation of the labeling process was developed by the author in order to pull together the strands of this potentially powerful theory of social motivation. Note that the focus of the theory is not merely on the process of stereotyping, though that is certainly involved. Rather, the focus is on the *effects* of the process for the individual's future motivation. These effects do not come about automatically. They depend on the acceptance by the individual, or his personal definition of the situation. Furthermore, the labels given to him may be positive or negative, good or bad, conscious or unconscious, verbal or nonverbal. Nonverbal labeling of a person may be based for example upon his dress, appearance, gestures, dialect or jargon. And the label may also be communicated without words. The nine steps of labeling are as follows:

1.   In the beginning there is some **initial action** by a person (or possibly by a group). This initial action is somehow notable or unique, but potentially falls into a pattern of behavior. The action may be deviant or normal. But it soon leads to **primary labeling** (Lemert) of this primary action. Other people label the individual or his action as notable or unique. They typify his action. The actor however does not yet label himself.

2.   More specifically, other people label the individual in *private*. They label him as individuals or in small subgroups, or ingroups. He is perhaps labeled by his intimates only at this point in time. First they label his *act* as a type or potential type of behavior governed by some social rule. His action is considered either deviance or notable normality.

3.   Others not only label the actor's action, in private, but they begin to label the *actor himself* as a person. They may refer to his self-image as a member of a type or class. These labels, in turn, may weaken or strengthen his current or former self image, opening it up to change or reinforcement.

4.   Next, the labeling by others of the act and/or actor becomes *public*. He is labeled by out-groups, such as neighbors, authorities, courts, etc., which strengthens the private labeling.

5.   We come now to the **typical action** which, if successful, is accepted by the subject. By a typical action we refer to a pattern or type of action intended by the actor. He is at least presumed to accept the pattern at this point. This self-labeling, or **secondary labeling** (Lemert) involves the subject's labeling of *himself* according to the purported type.

6.   First he *privately* labels *his own act* as one of the type. In his own mind he assents, or he admits his pattern to ingroups only. If, however, he considers the action deviant, he "neutralizes" it. He may a) deny responsibility for the deviant act. b) He may deny that there was any injury done. c) He may deny the victim, or the

victim's claim to any other treatment. d) He may condemn the condemners of his actions. e) Or, he may appeal to a higher loyalty (Sykes and Matza). On the other hand, if the actor considers his action acceptable, important, or good, he will likely reinforce it in his own mind by praising it, even by showing reverence for it, certainly by repeating it, or by enjoying or reveling in the act and its effects.

7.   After labeling his own action according to the type, the actor may then *privately* label *himself* or his person as a whole as one of the type. In other words, *he accepts the label*, whether deviant or normal.

8.   Then the actor uses the label as a **motive.** He uses the label as a reason or rationalization for acting in the typical manner. In this crucial step, the typical pattern of actions has now in a sense become part of his career pattern.

9.   Finally, the actor labels himself and his actions in *public*. In the presence of outgroups or outsiders, he proclaims his actions and himself as a person as one of the type, which confirms him in the pattern.

These nine steps may not occur in order. Some of them may not occur at all for a particular person experiencing the process. And many steps may simply be implied. But in the ideal typical case, these steps comprise the essence of labeling theory.

Example

■ Illustrations could be given for labeling someone into innumerable roles, such as delinquent, criminal, dumbbell, bright student ("brain"), radical, conformist, athlete, liberated woman, etc. Here we shall give a step-by-step analysis of the effects of labeling on a "foreigner" or stranger.

1.   The initial action of the person may be going to work temporarily in a foreign country without mastering the language, perhaps as a guest worker.

2.   His fellow workers tab him as foreign because he speaks little and with a heavy accent.

3.   Because of the difficulty of communicating with him, they soon give him a more permanent labeling not only because of his language. His personality as a whole, whether true or not, becomes isolated from all but one or two of his most patient fellow workers.

4.   He becomes in effect publicly labeled as the foreigner, not only by his fellow workers, but by those who live in the same rooming house, by sales clerks and waitresses, bus drivers, in

short, by almost everyone with whom he comes in contact.

5.   With all of this reinforcement, he cannot help but become fixed in his ways of dealing with others. Noncommunication is the worst form of punishment (whether intended or not) and so leads easily to the visitor labeling himself as a true foreigner, as one not accepted into his new environment.

6.   He sees his own speech patterns and consequent behavior as strange, even unacceptable, but unavoidable for him.

7.   He now even believes he is a true character type, a bit weird, a stranger.

8.   He uses the label to justify avoiding contact with other people, and for getting out of certain kinds of undesirable work.

9.   He even tells the boss he cannot accept a more responsible position as leader over a group of fellow workers because he cannot communicate well enough to control them. He has taken a relatively final step toward maintaining his role of foreigner. He seems destined to obscurity, no matter how technically competent he is on the job. He has publicly labeled himself.   ■

See *Recommended Reading and Study Questions* in Appendix, beginning on page 166.

Chapter 15

Dramaturgy

Erving Goffman is a profoundly insightful observer of everyday social encounters. Looking at life as theater, he helps us with his concepts to see not only what happens **front stage** and is portrayed to the audience, but also what happens in the informal system, in the **backstage** regions between the members of the **performance team.** He shows us how the actors and all people construct a performance for both the **audience** and the team by **managing their impressions,** maintaining a certain distance from their manifest role, and playing or enacting such **discrepant roles** as informer, shill, detective, go-between, nonperson, service specialist, confidant, or colleague. Such insights take on new dimensions inside **total institutions** such as prisons, insane asylums, convents, where the inmates eat, sleep, and work in common, under a regime of specific rules. In fact, a look into such institutions allows us to better see the inner workings of human nature, including some of the cruelties we inflict upon one another, usually without reflecting on them. In the process of looking, we can find out how it is possible, and then how we typically go about trying to change our neighbor.

Dramaturgy has strong theoretical ties to, and flows naturally out of some basic concepts of symbolic interactionism, such as roles, role-taking, and definition of the situation. The perspective's insights and concepts are primarily helpful in focusing on certain types of problematic interaction. However, it is possible to explicitly state some hypotheses which are only implicit in the original writing. One of the most central hypotheses or assumptions of dramaturgy is that: *Members of a performance team play discrepant roles in order to manage the impression the audience receives of them in order to achieve some team goals which are opposed to those of the audience.*

Examples

■ An informer (a type of discrepant role player) may be a spy who in fact joins a group as though he believed in its principles when in fact he believes the opposite. A narcotics agent may manage his impression and pose as a long-haired hippie type in his front stage behavior. He does so in order to gain the confidence of illegal drug users, pushers or a narcotics ring. After he gains the evidence needed to make a conviction he reports it (in the back stage region) to the proper authorities (the team) and disappears from the drug scene. The authorities may eventually make arrests, or wait until they gain additional evidence about other ring leaders from other informers. ■

Agent provocateurs have been known to join groups of peace demonstrators in order to lead them or provoke them into riot for political purposes. The guilty persons other than the agent provocateur himself will then quickly be arrested. He as a member of the performance team of law enforcement officers, managed his impression to the audience, the demonstrators themselves, in order to induce them into displaying their illegal backstage behavior. The backstage area here is the scene of the lawbreaking, while the front stage action is the peace demonstration. Incidentally, the legality of the agent provocateur's role is seriously questionable.

See *Recommended Reading and Study Questions* in Appendix, beginning on page 168.

Chapter 16

Ethnomethodology

Harold Garfinkel is the prophet of this newest approach to sociology at a micro level. Radically different from other approaches, its proponents are highly critical of almost all other theories and methodological procedures. They use a kind of dialectical approach, gathering ethnographic data, especially at the level of two-person conversations. They make the highly pertinent observation that other approaches fail to consciously seek to explain the ultimate social psychological question: *How does social order develop?* Considering traditional loyalties and communication patterns among certain groups of social scientists, this school of thought is a deepening and a specification of dramaturgy in an attempt to develop more general philosophical hypotheses. The message of **ethnomethodology** for the investigator can be tentatively stated in terms of the following rules for valid and reliable research: The investigator of social interaction must describe and explain the phenomena of social interaction from the point of view of, and in the manner and words and in the context of the **interactors** (the people being studied). The **preconscious rules** or usually hidden assumptions of social interaction should be looked at, preferably by using some variation on "the *documentary method of interpretation*." The focus of interest should be on the emergence or appearance of **rules** of social interaction, or the way by which a sense of social order emerges in the perceptions of the subjects. The **task** is to isolate the general types of interpersonal techniques that people employ in interaction, such as the following three:

1. **"Searching for the normal form"** (see Cicourel, *Cognitive Sociology*) is a method used by interacting persons when they sense ambiguity in their vision of the "normal" form for their

situation, or for their interaction patterns. When this happens the persons indicate to one another that they need to return to what is "normal" for that context.

2. "Doing a **reciprocity of perspectives**" means that actors presume and indicate to one another that if they were to switch places they would have the same experiences.

3. "Using the **Et Cetera Principle**" begins with the realization that much is left "unsaid" in interaction. The actors agree not to disrupt by asking for the missing information. They "wait for" it. When they "fill in" information in this way they are using the "et cetera principle."

Although Garfinkel does not explicitly say so, the following guidelines flow out of or are natural extensions of his procedures. In the process of describing and explaining the phenomenon under investigation, the investigator should examine its past and its probable future, as well as its present. He should look at both the public and formal system as well as the private, backstage phenomena (in the spirit of Erving Goffman). The researcher should also spell out his own assumptions, his own history, present life situation, his interest in the phenomenon under study, including his immediate social situation and societal factors influencing him. It would be more provocative if he could do this in the manner of a Socratic dialogue, which has kinship with the documentary method of interpretation. In the process the writer should make a case both for his guiding hypothesis as well as for its refutation, always pointing to possible revisions of the hypothesis.

The "documentary method of interpretation" consists of the analysis and interpretation of two-party conversations, using a two-column format. The **dialogue** is stated in the left column, the observer–scientist-writer's **interpretation** in the right column. This approach is exceptionally helpful to the reader in that it does not restrict itself, as do the vast majority of journal articles, to the abstracted data and conclusions. Rather, it gives the original script, as it were, and allows the reader to draw his own conclusions both about the content as well as about the interpretation of the original writer or scientific analyst. This brings in that element of Socratic dialogue, or **dialectical conversation** between the four major parties involved in an observational study, namely: 1) the first person in the original conversation, 2) the second person in the original conversation, 3) the observer-writer, and 4) the reader. It is hoped, with good reason, that this method will provide the range of materials, tools, assumptions, goals and interpretive processes necessary to deeper insight as well as more rapid advance of the enterprise of social science. The goal of philosophical generalization about the social order and interaction process between persons is a noble one, but rarely achieved in practice.

Example

■ "The documentary method of interpretation" is demonstrated in the following dialogue, which was taken from a paper written by social psychology student Edna Elizabeth McCutchen. This example is intended to be typical or representative, rather than complete or definitive. Notice how the degree of common understanding between the two parties cannot be measured, even on so limited a topic. Here we have an ordinary exchange between a husband and wife about one of the two daily papers to which they subscribe:

WIFE: Did you get the paper this morning?

Was it delivered early enough for you to read it before you went to work? Was it delivered at the door or thrown out on the terrace? There has been difficulty with this delivery.

HUSBAND: I bought one downtown.

It wasn't here when I left for work, or I didn't see it, and I certainly didn't look for it all over the yard.

WIFE: I called them yesterday.

I called the newspaper office and told them that it was not being delivered at all, or too late, etc.

HUSBAND: You can cancel it for me.

I would just as soon buy it on the newsstand, but I know you may not find this an agreeable plan.

WIFE: Oh, I hate to cancel it.

In the first place, it's too expensive to buy it every day—and then sometimes you take the other morning paper with you and there wouldn't be a paper here to read in the morning. Also, we have health insurance with that paper.

HUSBAND: Do whatever you like.

I don't know why she wants to waste the time trying to improve the delivery when I can bring the paper home with me. I wouldn't need to take the other one with me.

WIFE: I'll call again this morning and ask for the carrier's name.

I'll call the carrier and try to secure his cooperation and then he won't lose his job through having so many complaints.

HUSBAND: Alright.

It probably won't do much good but if she wants to try, let her. I wouldn't spend the time or trouble, but if she wants to, I won't say anything against it. ■

From this dialogue one can infer many philosophical generalizations about the emergence of social order in the minds of the participants. For example, there is a strong underlying element of mutual trust which allows the conversation to proceed without bewilderment, annoyance, or anger. More is implied than actually spoken, indicating the use of the "et cetera principle." The actors make inferences from what is left unspoken, as well as from what was actually said. The sequence of statements indicates that both partners thought about the problem beforehand. They both expected a normal resolution of the issue. Despite some disagreement on how to handle the situation, they were both ready to "search for the normal form" or the normal interaction pattern over their mutual problem. They referred to one another's biographies in the process of their search. They saw things from the point of view of the other person, thus engaging in a "reciprocity of perspectives." One could even make practical inferences about the wife being more concerned about economic matters, but the husband retaining the final decision-making power. Both are concerned with the current news. The husband rises early, but sometimes the wife sleeps later. The wife would not want anyone to lose their job if it were possible for her to prevent it. The social order portrayed is likely a microcosm of their entire relationship.

See *Recommended Reading and Study Questions* in Appendix, beginning on page 169.

Critique of
Social Interaction Theories

REVIEW AND COMPARISON

The reader should at this point review the comparative ideas in the introduction to Part V, along with the separate introductions to Chapters 13 through 16 (treating symbolic interactionism, labeling, dramaturgy and ethnomethodology). It should be clear that the social interaction theories are all focused primarily on social *process* rather than social *structure*, as such. Dramaturgy, of the four, appears to concentrate most on a loosely integrated set of descriptive concepts, which almost inevitably leads it to play up the structural elements at the expense of process concepts. In practice, to explain change or process implies the prior or simultaneous explanation (not just description) of the structural elements of an ongoing, interacting group or society. Process explanations are thus inevitably more difficult to give because to be complete, they must explain not only the process of change but also the structure of the group or society under consideration. A developmental explanation (e.g., Chapter 2) is also difficult because it covers the entire lifetime of a human being. The interactionist type of explanations are especially useful in explaining such things as the relation of a person to his group or society, or how a number of members of a society can act separately, but with a common goal of changing aspects of their society. Interactionist explanations also suggest how for example a number of members of society can try to achieve self-actualization in their own sphere of life, and how the cumulative effect of such attempts can amount to or lead to the formation of a social movement (as a type of collective behavior). Examples in much of present-day western society include the encounter group movement, the new quasi-religious and actual religious movement back to fundamentalist and Oriental forms such as the Jesus freaks, the underground church, Hare Krishna, Zen and Nichiren Shoshu varieties of Buddhism; Yoga, and also Alphawave machines to measure whether one is in a meditative state, and the recent return to meditation as a means to, as well as a sign of fulfillment.

If enough members of a society become members of a particular type of new social movement, that society can certainly be said to be in a process of changing structures. When the new structures become generally accepted and followed, that social movement is then said to be institutionalized. Such a society has then clearly undergone significant social change. An explanation of such change could be given without difficulty within the framework of symbolic interactionism. It could also rather easily be done, at least in partial ways, by exchange theory and role bargaining. The use of many other social psychological theories could well explain certain aspects of such collective behavior and institutionalization. But each separate explanation would only be partial.

In the moderately long run it is still not practicable without significant new theoretical breakthroughs to be satisfied with an explanation of a social problem or issue based on only one theory, even on symbolic interactionism. To do so is to limit one's explanation severely, and even to ultimately hold back the progress of social psychology by being satisfied with partial and fragmentary explanations which are useful or only expedient for the moment or for the scientist's present piece of research. A program of comparative research based on widely differing groups of theories seems called for. It is asking a rather higher degree of discipline than most social scientists are accustomed to in their work. But this author sees no other immediately feasible way to advance the field significantly toward a more general or synthetic theory. As far as the individual student is concerned, practically the same precaution should be given. Do not be satisfied with an explanation in terms of one theory alone. It may take a bit more time and energy to explain one's problem with the hypotheses of two or three theories taken separately. But the attempt and the resulting comparison should be provocative in itself and give us a fuller understanding of the social world. And who knows? Maybe the idea will catch on and eventually be systematically employed by professional social psychologists. If so, the field will have moved forward a significant step in the direction of more general theories.

In particular, the structuralist, behaviorist, and congruency sets of theories are typically used in a far too ad hoc and momentary fashion to be very useful for achieving the long range primary goal of general explanation. To dismiss this goal altogether is foolhardy, defeatist, and highly limiting in its effects on the researcher as well as the student. The needs of students, especially the nonspecialist or nonmajor are also for deeper, more general explanations. On this score, can we not then truthfully say that what is good for students is good for social psychology?

Evaluation and Application of Symbolic Interactionism

Symbolic interactionism favors the inductive, case study approach, although its propositions are generally amenable to deductive reorientation, a condition which is aided by the richness of its propositions. It is easy to apply in a partial way, but requires a considerable amount of thought to apply in detail, again because of the richness of its array of concepts. It thus has very high information value. When it is applied in detail, it has very high explanatory power. But due to its fluidity, general vagueness, and here-and-now character, it has relatively weak predictability. A great deal of empirical support has been forthcoming. But due to the difficulty of applying it in detail, owing to its richness, much more research needs to be done to test this metatheory in a systematic way.

To change a person with symbolic interaction, we should by gestures indicate what we want them to do, or what they should do. If they then accurately take our role and define the situation as favorable to our goal for them, then they will attempt to achieve it. This will depend in part on any impulses, past experience and what their "me," considers to be proper behavior in that situation.

Example

■ A gesture by a policeman may indicate that we should wait at a street intersection despite the fact that we have the green light. Our law-abiding "Me" acting on our proper definition of the situation tells us what is proper, namely, to wait for the policeman's signal to proceed. Our trained behavior is changed to this extent by the policeman in a continuing process of symbolic interaction. In fact, every imaginable situation involving change (or stability) of behavior can ultimately be attributed to internal controls (the "I"-"Me" process), in the context of the person's definition of the situation. This includes everyday conversation, grocery shopping, driving, playing tennis, undergoing psychoanalysis, or making war or peace. ■

To achieve self-actualization aided by symbolic interactionism we should by reflection, come to an understanding of our self-concept as a whole with a view to full development of the self. We should instruct our "Me" to appropriately censure contrary impulses. We should gesture or communicate to others, especially to significant others, our long range goal of actualization, and solicit help and support from them in achieving it. All possible situations we encounter should be defined as potentially self-actualizing situations, and pragmatically used as such, or accordingly enjoyed.

Example

■ Such a general theory as symbolic interactionism does not give specific directives. But it does allow us to develop our own specific subtheory. Every person we meet who is receptive and seems insightful, or is himself actualized can be a help to us. We must only try to be open to his personal light by taking the risk of opening up our deeper feelings to him. Reflection upon our self-concept and our life situation, occupation, and desired future life will help us select the appropriate plan of action for fuller day-to-day living. There are elements of such a plan which are common to religious conversation. A new and better way of life appears on the horizon, captures our imagination, and then takes hold of us in a revolutionary way. St. Paul was knocked off his horse. Ignatius of Loyola felt strong attraction in his conversion to a life of service to his church. He also showed how the normal calling is based on meditative planning. The lives of such great men as Albert Schweitzer and Mahatma Gandhi are also beautiful examples of a call of thoughtful men to self-actualization by means of working for social or societal actualization. ■

Evaluation and Application of Labeling

The labeling perspective has been developed inductively from participant observation and case studies. Its followers typically start their research with participant observation of interesting informal settings, such as dance halls, parties, bars, playgrounds, mental hospitals, and other groups or relationships of a relatively long-term, on-going nature. Labeling generally occurs over a significant period of time, long enough for the label to stick to, and then sink into the self-concept of its recipient. Otherwise it would not likely be effective in producing change or molding its victim or beneficiary, as the case may be.

Concerning the four criteria for a good theory, if the period of time under consideration is too short, this perspective does not apply well. It is also more difficult to apply if the subject does not accept the label. However, if it does apply, then, as per the nine-point sequence, it gives us concepts of high information value. It helps us to describe what happened, over time, to the central person. It is less valuable however in explaining just *why* the events happened the way they did. It might help us to predict a labeled person's future behavior once he had clearly accepted the label, but would not normally be very useful in predicting whether or not a person in the initial stages would later accept a label and make it his own. The circumstances of the specific application of the perspective, of course, will modify these general evaluations. Finally, it should be noted that empirical support for the theory is large, but heavily ad hoc and common-sense rather than systematic.

To change a person using the labeling perspective, it would simply be necessary to label him and his actions, privately and publicly, in the way we want him to be. If we do it gradually and subtly enough, know how to overcome the resistance and rationalizations of our client or subject, in most instances we will be successful. Of course, we will need support from his other significant relatives and friends. So this is a big undertaking, at least if the change desired is to eventually reach the depths of his self-concept.

Example

■ How can one change a high-school girl who is a lonely wallflower type? Informal experiments have shown that her male classmates must get together and begin dating her frequently. Her former self-label of "wallflower" will soon be changed almost inevitably to something like "popular girl." And all the self-definitions that go with it will be changed. The private labeling of the boys, however contrived in the beginning, will become public, then be accepted privately and publicly by the girl as really true of her behavior and even of her self-concept as a whole. ■

A person could begin to move himself to self-actualization by labeling himself in progressive, attainable stages, up the ladder toward his goal. A positive attitude about oneself will lead others to reaffirm it. A radical reversal of one's basic personality traits is however not likely to come about with ease nor very quickly—popular success manuals to the contrary. Nor is there any easy, overnight way to get oneself labeled as a self-actualizing person. But the obvious first step is to make a genuine effort to achieve it, which includes labeling oneself as self-actualizing. Private acceptance of the label will normally be followed by public recognition of it in particular instances of behavior, and then as regards our person as a whole. A change in our attitude to life is bound to be noticed by our close contacts who, once they have accepted our new life goals, will inevitably reinforce our self-label of actualization seeker.

Example

■ The various individual forms of actualization are so diverse as to defy classification. However, the most obvious forms are also closely related to the person's notable service to society, to his participation in community, or in other words, to his work for social actualization. These are the saints and public heroes, the courageous politicians and citizens of our time. Ralph Nader (the citizen-consumer action organizer) would be one. Whether you agree or not with his action, Daniel Ellsberg was acting courageously to defend a principle of freedom from government censorship of news when he released the Pentagon Papers on the conduct of the Vietnam War to the general public. The long and arduous trial that followed demonstrates the great personal sacrifice that was required. Presumably this was the path to his self-and social actualization in his circumstances at the time. This list of heroes and great men and women of history is long. Every reader will have his own model person. Our problem, however, is still to get ourself labeled, not as a hero, but as a person fulfilled, a constant contributor to a better society for all. Finally, we must ourselves believe in our own personal worth. ■

Evaluation and Application of Dramaturgy

The dramaturgical perspective begins with the stage as a *model*, but in practice its researchers use a decidedly inductive approach to theory construction. They observe settings with some concepts in mind, and then try to relate their observations in terms of the stage model. In fact, it is difficult to even develop explicit hypotheses with dramaturgy since the concepts are not well integrated. It provides more of an analogy than an explicit theory. It is easy to apply in natural settings. Because of the insightfulness of its concepts, it has high information value. However, it is very weak on predictability and explanatory power. Empirical support is vague since its followers use the case approach in a heuristic way rather than to systematically test the perspective as a theory.

To change a person with dramaturgy, manage your impression, put on a performance with a team, or if necessary, play discrepant roles in order to con him into doing what you want. Work the system, using one's powers of deception and persuasion in both the front and backstage regions. If nothing else works, create a closed environment, a total institution for the person you are trying to change so that he might be more easily stripped of his former self and manipulated or conditioned into doing what you want him to do.

Example

■ To change the boss, or the customer, or to succeed in the business world, one must be careful to whom he admits his real feelings about work problems. Any negative reflection on working conditions or the boss's way of making decisions must never be spoken in public, or in the front stage region. The image of the company presented to customers and all but the most liberal of bosses must be positive, even if it means secrecy, playing a discrepant role, such as service specialist. The customer is the audience, fellow workers the performance team. The team serves the public, say by manufacturing furniture. The furniture has a beautiful appearance but may not be of the sturdiest quality. The salesman must admit the lesser quality only to fellow workers, team members, or other company men in the backstage region. In order to sell the product he must manage his impression to the customer, so the customer will buy the product and also be proud to show it off to his friends. A successful furniture sale is a sign of a kind of change of mind of the customer from that of potential to actual buyer. ■

To attain self-actualization with dramaturgy, we should use deception only when our better selves consider it appropriate, say as etiquette or in institutionalized discrepant roles. Otherwise, more honest behavior seems called for. In a way, it seems that fulfillment is more likely to occur when behavior characteristic of the back stage region comes more closely into line with front stage behavior.

Example

■ I cannot be true to my inner self when I have to compromise my principles to keep my job. I may hold a civil service job under a politically rightist administration. If my real principles of life are liberal, I will eventually be called to speak my principles publicly in opposition to the administration, even at the risk of losing my job. I need not be blatant or obnoxious. In fact, I had better be tactful and

keep within my sound legal rights as a citizen. If I am fortunate enough
to live in a truly democratic country I can show my opposition
without fear of losing my job. Under a nondemocratic regime, in order
to survive, I will have to mask my true feelings, perhaps admitting
them only among trusted friends, say in an underground opposition
party meeting. Self and social actualization can only really come
when a genuinely democratic regime is democratically instituted. Or I
must leave the country for a freer country. A celebrated case in point is
the exile from the Soviet Union of the opposition author, Aleksandr
Solzhenitsyn. ■

Evaluation and Application of Ethnomethodology

Ethnomethodology uses a highly inductive approach, though when
the documentary method is used properly, it falls into the functional
mode of theory building. It is thus receptive to continual revision of
theory through the interplay with data in an ongoing cycle of
hypothesizing and testing. It is easy to apply to conversations, but is
difficult for the average student to make observations that are highly
significant. This depends primarily on the sophistication of the
observer and/or researcher. Its information value, per se, is very
limited, as is its predictability. Its explanatory power, per se, is
limited, but is open in a productive way to remarkable insights into
everyday encounters. Empirical support is slim, but mounting in very
recent years. However, the fact that this approach is more a method
than a theory makes judgments of this kind only marginally relevant.

Since this is primarily a methodological approach, it does not
give us hypotheses that might help to change a person, or to achieve
actualization.

SAMPLE COMPARATIVE WRITE-UP

Theater Play Analyzed With Exchange and Symbolic Interactionism

The reader should here again review the plot summary of the play
Angel Street in the Student Use section after Part II on p. 55.

Exchange Applied

To review, exchange theory is based on the ultimate equation Profit =
Reward − Cost. Rewards and costs must be assessed or computed as
far as possible from the point of view of the actor or person under

investigation or scientific observation. Since this is practically impossible, the researcher must make the best estimate he can in order to decide whether and to what degree the interaction or relationship under consideration is profitable for the subject person. It is useful to divide up the action sequence into segments, before and after some crucial event.

The mental tortures endured by Mrs. Manningham are obviously costs for her. Her husband and one of the servants help to pressure her in trying ways. She does receive some rewards, but they are of less value than the costs, indicating that either her relationship with him is threatened, or, as is the case, her mental and emotional health is in jeopardy. She is happy at going to the theater with him, and enjoys serving tea and muffins, a small consolation in the face of the insidiousness of his treachery.

The crucial intervening event again is the visit of the benign police inspector who drops in one afternoon while Mr. Manningham is out of the house. After the inspector enlightens her, she is greatly relieved and thereby rewarded by the discovery of the truth and the reaffirmation of her sanity. The cost for her, if it can be considered such, is the loss of her husband (who is not legally married to her anyway because he still has an abandoned wife in a foreign country). The overall profit for her is her justification and freedom from torments, surely a more desirable situation than the one existing at the earlier point in time, at the beginning of the play. A similar evaluation could be made of the rewards and costs for Mr. Manningham, but for the sake of brevity, that will be left to the initiative of the reader.

Symbolic Interactionism Applied

The social act is central to symbolic interactionism. Very simply, Mr. Manningham gestures to her (in a broad sense of that term) to indicate or insinuate that she is mad (e.g., by accusing her of unknowingly moving a picture from the wall). She in turn takes his role, and interprets with trepidation, fear, and need of support, doubting her own sanity. Her gesture in response to his insinuation is to swear on the Bible that she did not do the things he accused her of (such as moving the picture from the wall). His gesture in response is to try to isolate her, to send her to her room alone, to refuse to discuss the matter openly with her, thus further insinuating that she is mad. He has attempted to cast her in the role of madwoman by so defining the situation for her, both by his direct actions and by circumscribing her round of life to this one old Victorian house. Her self-concept is weakened by his onslaught, but she remains uncertain until the truth comes out in new social actions with the police inspector. In the beginning her "I" is confused and upset, while her "Me" is merely upset over his insinuations which she sees as false. From the standpoint of her generalized other, she does not identify her circumstances immediately with those of her mother, but rather with the normal life's role that she had been playing until now, with the forces for justice embodied in the older servant, Elizabeth, and later in the police inspector.

Some hypotheses in the symbolic interactionist tradition (from Shibutani and Kwan: 1965) also fit the main action. *Consensus is facilitated by the use of common communication channels.* A degree of consensus about her insanity occurs between Mr. Manningham and the young servant, Nancy, because Mrs. Manningham's communication channels with the outside world are so narrowly restricted. When the channels are interrupted by the entrance on the scene of the police inspector and accompanying new communication channels, there is no longer consensus among a majority about her insanity. More specifically, *patterns of concerted action persist as long as communication channels remain unchanged.* The action to drive her insane persists until the police inspector enlightens her.

Evaluation of Application of Exchange and Symbolic Interactionism

Exchange theory is easy to apply because it requires knowledge of only two basic concepts, reward and cost. If our interpretations of the subject person are accurate, then we need only evaluate the relative merits or weighting of the two concepts in order to compute the profit for that person. The difficulty in *Angel Street* is to decide what is rewarding for Mrs. Manningham. Her happiness at the beginning is only momentary, that of going to the theater and then serving her husband. Her costs are the suffering of accusations and insinuations that she is insane. There is little relative profit for her, at least until she finds out the truth about her husband.

Symbolic interactionism is also quite easy to apply, especially to this kind of two-person interaction. The major gestures and role-taking processes are clear because of the limited boundaries of the action. The relevance of her self-concept is apparent. Her internal confusion can easily be imputed to discern what is happening in her internalized conversation of gestures between her "I" and her "Me." As for the hypotheses illustrated, it is not difficult to pick out examples of consensus (about her insanity), communication channels (with the outside world), and patterns of concerted action (her husband and his use of the servant Nancy to help drive her insane).

Some judgment naturally had to be used in order to limit the application to the two specific hypotheses mentioned. This is a possible overall difficulty, or locus of possible error in interpretation. But then observer judgment is always a source of invalidity in social research.

The information value of exchange theory is only average because of its severely limited number of basic terms, though the basic equation does facilitate our cognitive understanding of each episode or scene on limited, but crucial variables. Information value of symbolic interaction is above average, better than exchange theory because of its wide range of concepts and at least implicit hypotheses. The concepts of definition of the situation, role taking, and communication channels are especially useful for the present story because they direct us to focus on methods used and the conditions determining the success of the attempt to drive Mrs. Manningham crazy. Exchange theory is limited, as stated, to an analysis of this crucial action in terms of a cost to her as an individual.

The predictability of either theory here is average at best. Exchange theory allows us to predict Mrs. Manningham's actions only after the police inspector reveals the plot to her, but not before. Until then we are kept in suspense. Until then she has no reward for suspecting her husband. Symbolic interactionism with its focus on the definition of the situation does not allow us to predict beyond the space of a few minutes or a few lines, because it is not yet specific enough. It is not a true theory but only a frame of reference, as are almost all theories.

The explanatory power of both theories is above average. Mrs. Manningham's perceived profit in remaining married, trusting her husband, and her relative isolation from the outside world, or additional sources of consensual support, explain rather pointedly why she did not suspect her husband's intentions before the police inspector entered the picture. Again, the notion in symbolic interactionism of the definition of the situation explains her naivete about equally as well as the reward-cost model, for all practical purposes.

Overall Evaluation of the Two Theories

Based in part on the application of exchange and symbolic interactionism to the concrete case, it is useful to attempt an overall assessment of the relative merit of the two perspectives as such. Exchange theory is probably the easiest of any perspective to apply to an almost unlimited number of situations. It is nearly universally applicable, which contributes to its outstanding degree of explanatory power. In situations with a limited number of variables operating, it has moderate information value and high predictive potential. However, its applicability is limited due to the difficulty of quantifying rewards and costs based on the inevitable lack of complete knowledge of persons and their situations. We can thus predict only after many imputations of the subjects' perceptions of rewards and costs. Information value of the theory is limited for the most part to what can be described in terms of the three major concepts. As for explanatory power, emotions and sentiments as motivators are only indirectly importable into the theory of why the subject acted as he did.

Symbolic interactionism, except as interpreted by a very few writers, lacks specific hypotheses. Thus, its ease of application is limited in its present stage of development. It is also a highly judgmental decision on how to specify each concept, vague as they are (however true to reality). It is easy to apply in a partial way, but requires a considerable amount of thought to apply in detail because of the richness of its array of concepts. It fails to predict the direction of long-term change due to its fluidity, indefinite, and here-and-now character. The vagueness of the concepts may well represent the truth of real life, and the breadth and number of concepts of symbolic interactionism gives it relatively high information value in most applications. Explanatory power of this theory is imperfect because of the lack of specificity of the concepts and hypotheses. But when these basic notions of the theory are applied carefully, and in detail, the explanatory power of symbolic interactionism is outstanding among extant sociological or social psychological theories.

Conclusion:
A Synthesis of Social
Psychological Theories

This chapter will first classify the sixteen contemporary theoretical perspectives of social psychology by their ordinary disciplinary domain, namely, either a) sociology, b) psychology, or c) social psychology proper. A second classification concerns the typical research application, approach to studying human behavior, or the type of task engaged in by the social scientist, namely, a) theorizing, b) empirical research, or c) participant observation. Then the most basic concepts and hypotheses of each perspective are related to a simple flow diagram in the mode of **general systems** theory (GST) in order to demonstrate the possibility for a larger synthesis of the various separate perspectives. The great number of disparate ad hoc perspectives of social psychology are in need of such synthesizing to give the discipline more breadth and generalizability to real life situations. Finally, a brief characterization of the perspectives (in their five groupings) is given in order to present an overview and draw out the implied model of man in a relationship.

In order to begin to better understand the interrelationships between and among the sixteen perspectives, it is helpful to locate them within their relevant subject matter fields. Three fields of study are pertinent here: sociology, psychology and social psychology. Strictly speaking, *sociology* deals with social organization and institutions, patterns of relationships between aggregates, collectivities, groups and societies. *Psychology* deals primarily with what goes on inside the person as a separate individual, or at least his individual behavior. *Social psychology* is somewhat of a bridge between the other two, though it is analytically separable. It deals with the person in a group. It may deal with individuals or with an already developed

FIGURE A

Disciplinary Domains

society or social system. But more often it looks at the interaction which occurs in the social situation, its origin, and the ongoing process.

Figure A locates the sixteen perspectives in tentative fashion in the three domains. Depending on the particular application of each perspective and the concepts which are emphasized in that application, the perspective might be located in a different position in the domain chart. Hence, the positioning of each is and will remain tentative.

Sociological

The interparty conflict perspective as treated here is predominantly sociological because it deals with the outcomes, social patterns, and functions that result from conflict between members of a group or society. This is the only perspective of the sixteen which I would classify as predominantly sociological in the strictest sense.

Psychological

Several perspectives are predominantly psychological, because their starting point for analysis is inside the person. Cognitive dissonance begins analysis in the cognitive realm, which may produce behavioral change in the individual. Symmetry, although involving communication between two people, focuses primarily on affect between the parties, their attitudes, and their change in attitude toward the attitude object. All these variables except communication are individual and therefore psychological. Self-consistency begins with concepts about the self and leads to a consideration of factors in individual change. According to this perspective, other people are brought in only through the self. Interpersonal congruence deals with a person's self-concept and self-image on an issue, but brings in other people only insofar as they have opinions about the person, and only as viewed by that subject person. Interpersonal congruence then has elements of the social situation, or the social psychological realm, but is still primarily psychological in its major terms. Stimulus-response behaviorism focuses on external behavior as filtered through the human organism, but treats other people mainly as stimuli to be responded to. The social aspects of situations tend to be viewed as closed systems, highly predetermined for the acting individual. S-R is a par excellence psychological perspective.

Social Psychological

A couple of perspectives are predominantly social psychological in the strict sense of dealing with the person in a situation. Group dynamics (including the notions of the reference group and the primary group) deals with persons in groups. It does not treat the individual alone, nor are its proponents usually interested in the structure of groups apart from the contribution and interpretation of the members. Ethnomethodology usually focuses on a two-person conversation, and hence is interactional. It deals with persons in an ongoing social situation. This is by definition a social psychological problem.

Combinations of Disciplines

Falling midway between the psychological and the social psychological realms are three perspectives. Labeling involves other people's labels given to the individual (a social psychological or situational factor) as well as the acceptance of the label or self labeling by the person (a psychological phenomenon). Dramaturgy deals with actors playing roles on stage, a social psychological occurrence. But, it also involves the discrepancy between the person's words and actions on the one hand, and his real intentions on the other. The real intentions are in the psychological realm. Symbolic interactionism is concerned with self and other, role taking and role enactment, definitions of the situation and gestures in conversations, and joint actions. These are a mixture of the psychological and social psychological together.

Directly in between all three realms fall three other perspectives. Exchange and game theory involve profits or outcomes, rewards and costs, which are either 1) situational or societal patterns, or 2) social organizational factors as viewed from the point of view of the individual person. Role bargaining is concerned with roles enacted or played out by individuals, in social situations, influenced by their obligations in their society and culture. Role bargaining is thus a strictly interdisciplinary perspective.

Three Task Roles of the Social Scientist

Figure B shows the three polar types of approach to studying human behavior. Two are procedures of data gathering: 1) **participant observation** and 2) **laboratory-controlled studies.** After data is gathered, or even while it is being gathered, the student of society must make sense out of it by developing a theory (the third polar construct in the diagram).

The corresponding types of study done by research oriented social scientists (as described by Bruyn: 1966) include the **traditional empiricist** who specializes in laboratory-controlled experimental and behavioral studies, and the **participant-observer** who engages in social and cultural studies. The ways of gathering data may be used in any combination, but the difficulties of expending time and energy in gathering information tend to lead each individual social scientist to use one main kind of approach to research. After his data are gathered, the researcher or some other social scientist must then try to develop a theory from that data. Of course, the researcher may, and inevitably does, begin his research with some kind of theory, at least an implicit one.

A theory, strictly speaking, is more than a conceptual system or taxonomy or classificatory scheme, frame of reference or paradigm. Rather, a **theory** is best viewed as a set of logically interrelated statements or hypotheses about the structures and social processes being studied. Unless the concepts are related in explanatory and

FIGURE B

Three Task Roles Of the Social Scientist

Theories
(Conceptual Systems)

General Systems

Symbolic
Interpersonal   Interactionism
Congruence
Conflict   Identity Development
                             Labeling

                Role Bargaining
Exchange, Game
                             Dramaturgy
        Group Dynamics   Ethnomethodology

Cognitive Dissonance
Symmetry   Self-Consistency
Stimulus-Response   Actualization
Behaviorism

Traditional Empiricist   **Participant-Observer**
(Experimental-Behavioral Studies   **(Social-Cultural Studies)**

predictive statements which are informative and falsifiable, the theory is perhaps only a conceptual scheme unrelated to the objectively observable social reality being studied. Anything less in our judgment is not a true theory. In addition, each particular theory itself has an inevitable bias toward some particular mode of approach to social scientific work. Each specific theory or each piece of research will then tend to fall somewhere between these three points of the task-role triangle.

Empiricism

Traditionally, the most empirical of all approaches is that of stimulus-response behaviorism. Because of their development out of this tradition (or out of an inclination toward laboratory-oriented small group studies, or the use of fixed-choice questionnaire surveys), the following social psychological theories fall very close to the traditional empiricist polar type: cognitive dissonance, symmetry, exchange, game theory, interpersonal congruence, and sometimes interparty conflict. Exchange and game theory, although having interdisciplinary possibilities, are most at home with laboratory research. All of these perspectives use a very limited number of concepts for analysis. Group dynamics usually also falls here, although some subordinate elements of it, namely reference groups and primary groups, are perhaps even more often treated by those using the methods of the participant observer.

Participant Observation

The perspectives which could be typified by their tendency toward the use of participant observation as an approach to research include actualization, self-consistency, labeling, dramaturgy, ethnomethodology, identity development and symbolic interaction. Role bargaining falls somewhere between the empiricist and the participant observer approaches, and is also somewhat more theoretical in its emphasis than most perspectives. Those who work with labeling and dramaturgy must rely on soft data, or observations made in natural settings. Otherwise, the artificiality of controlled settings, special rooms and observational equipment would obviate the possibility of seeing through to people's actual feelings, labels and intentions. The ethnomethodologist, while not necessarily present at the conversation being analyzed, nor necessarily a participant, typically analyzes the conversation by using a tape-recorded sequence, usually in a natural setting. Self-consistency is dependent upon interviews with counselees, and hence makes use of participant observation by the therapist, although the setting is usually somewhat artificial, being done from the therapist's armchair rather than in field observations. Identity development depends on long-term observations, perhaps personal documents and case material, letters and diaries, reminiscences of relatives, and interviews with the subject person. All these procedures are closer to participant observation than to laboratory research. Actualization, since it stresses authenticity and realness of people in their encounters with the deeper issues, can only with difficulty and remoteness be studied in the laboratory. Symbolic interactionism is most compatible with direct observation and the plausibility achieved by seeing the world through the thoughts and definitions of the situation made by that unique person in context.

Theoretical Approaches

Among these traditionally empiricist perspectives, the one most theoretically oriented in its statement and use is that of interpersonal congruence. This is so in part because it systematically brings into play several key notions and concepts from the other perspectives in the laboratory tradition. Among the perspectives which lean toward participant observation, the most theoretical is symbolic interactionism. The other perspectives make only relatively insightful use of concepts, techniques, procedures or ways of looking at the larger research picture. Social psychology is weakest at the level of grand or synthetic theory. Its tendency toward restricted laboratory work or concrete observations has led the field to ad hoc, limited, or at best middle-range theorizing. Symbolic interactionism is probably the most theoretical of social psychological approaches, although as a theory it is very incomplete. Its hypotheses are largely in the nature of assumptions, methodological directives, or implicit general propositions. It is most at home with participant observation as a research procedure, because of its focus on the person in a social situation who must continually redefine the situation as time progresses and conditions change.

Role bargaining is compatible with research in either the laboratory setting or the natural setting of the participant observer. Because it is global and abstract, I believe it has more potential for synthetic theory building than do most of the others, except for symbolic interactionism, which is the most complete, explanatory, and informative of any treated here (in my opinion). Exchange theory also has a high potential for synthesizing much research into a more comprehensive theory. Most of the other extant perspectives, at the present stage of development, have an unfortunately ad hoc character to them. This, it seems to me, is unlikely to lead to much real advance in the field of social science. However, it is my hope that general systems theory can be used to make such an advance. It can be employed as a metatheory to begin to synthesize, or at least show the overlapping and intertwining domains of the many smaller substantive perspectives. Still, it will take a great deal of additional work to piece together the details of a general systems synthesis.

General Systems as a Synthesizing Metatheory

Figure C is a flow diagram of the general process of a person or group acting and achieving effects on the environment and system (as treated by Walter Buckley, 1967: p. 173). Taking the key concepts of each perspective, one at a time, and plugging them into this simple but extremely basic diagram will be another way to help us visualize the overlapping provinces of each.

If we take the control center as the acting individual, we can see that his action outputs involve his unusual or notable behavior, which

FIGURE C

General Systems Flow Diagram

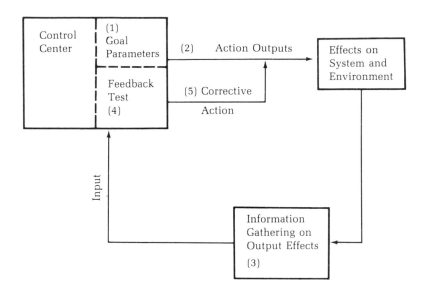

is labeled by others in the social system or group. When the subject person gathers information on the effect of his actions on the environment, he is likely to find that he is labeled in a way that types his behavior over a period of time, leading to expectations that he will repeat that behavior, and even identify himself as a type of person who does that kind of thing habitually. If the labeling is effective, if he accepts it, his corrective action over the long run will be in the direction of using that label to justify his future behavior of that type. Next, each of the sixteen theories or perspectives will be reviewed.

Psychological Perspectives

This section covers four congruency theories plus S-R behaviorism.

Cognitive dissonance is initiated somehow in the mind of the actor, probably from some feedback showing unfavorable effects of his actions on the environment. In order to resolve that dissonance he takes corrective action in the form of either changing his behavior (action outputs), or changing his ideas (goal parameters).

Symmetry is concerned with a person having positive feelings towards another person whose attitudes are different than his own.

The person will tend to then either bring his attitudes into line with the other's or become more negative in his feeling toward that other person.

Self-consistency is a device for guiding the person to look at his goals and test the feedback he receives against his hierarchy of goals. If there is inconsistency, then he will be expected to take corrective action against his usual action outputs in order to achieve the desired effect on the environment, or to bring the various elements of his self-concept into greater overall consistency.

Interpersonal congruence looks at the overall self-concept and the particular self-image on the issue (both being parts of the goal parameters). It then compares these to its feedback from the other person(s) involved. The tendency is to bring these three elements into line with one another, whether by changing his actions, i.e., taking corrective action in order to receive more favorable feedback, or else to change the self-image or even the overall self-concept of the actor.

S-R behaviorism of the classical conditioning variety involves association in the mind of the actor of the conditioned and the unconditioned stimuli so that either can produce the conditioned response. Operant conditioning involves reinforcement by others in the system of the action outputs of the subject. Effects desired by the experimenter are rewarded with positive feedback. Effects undesired by the experimenter in the subject are punished with negative feedback.

Sociological Perspectives

Interparty conflict as a perspective looks at conflict in the environment which produces clearer feedback or knowledge of the other party, which then allows the person or group to be more productive or achieve better relationships with the opposition, or at least to know how to handle or better cope with it, by taking corrective action.

Social Psychological Perspectives

The group dynamics perspective involves coming to terms with one's social system in the form of the groups he belongs to, as well as his reference groups and primary groups. The reference group, being simply another group as imagined, is thus centered in the control center. The primary group is by definition a real group, a part of the person's physical environment, which provides him with the primary feedback in his socialization into society. Group dynamics focuses on the attempt to make the individual deviant conform to the group or system norms through feedback to him about what is appropriate behavior in the laboratory situation.

Ethnomethodology zeroes in on the social order, how it originates, and is sustained through a process of continual corrective action and feedback from the environment, or other people in particular. The observer makes clear his biases and his interpretation of the conversation, which in turn helps to clarify the underlying rules or underlying latent goal parameters of the participants.

Combinations of Domain

This section covers eight theories.

Dramaturgy looks at the attempts of the person to con others or to fake them out by managing his impression, by acting in a way that will produce the desired effects on the others and work to the advantage of the person, regardless of the consistency achieved within himself, even if it requires playing discrepant roles.

Labeling theorists look primarily at the inputs into the individual (control center) in the form of other persons' labels of the individual and his behavior. If these labels are insistent enough and the individual does not have a strong enough self-concept, he will likely take corrective action to conform to the label the other has given to his previous pattern of behavior (action outputs). Eventually the individual may change his goal parameters to conform to the new labels. His self-labels (as part of his goal parameters) will then have come into line with the input received from the others' labels of him.

Exchange theory is concerned with the attempt to achieve more positive than negative feedback from one's action attempts.

Game theory requires the taking of corrective action after receiving feedback on outcomes of mutually interdependent choices, in order to achieve the desired goals, effects, or feedback.

Role bargaining can be viewed as the individual's attempts to reconcile the various role expectations made on him by his environment and past experience. He gathers information based on his present position and comes to terms with the conflict between roles in order to take whatever corrective action is necessary to better cope with the environment and people in his life and career.

Symbolic interactionism involves the gestures or action outputs of the person made to another, which has certain effects on the other. The return gestures of the other to the subject become the feedback gathered through the role-taking process. The self-concept is at the center of the control center of the person. His "Me" is developed through feedback from his effects on the environment. The "Me" corrects the impulsive tendency to act; the "I" leads to corrective action in the form of new gestures or overt actions.

Identity development involves a long-term series of corrective actions in order to develop the skills to cope with the changing environment of the person, including his self identity (which is at the center of his goal parameters).

Actualization focuses on the crucial life issues, the fulfillment of the potential of the control center as a whole integrated person, who continually must take corrective action to overcome the inhibiting effects of the environment on his authentic behavior. The need ladder is gradually climbed through a process of more accurate feedback in the light of more awareness of what goal parameters are more worthwhile.

With this brief review of all sixteen perspectives based on the general systems flow chart, I hope that the reader of these pages has come to a somewhat better grasp of how the sixteen perspectives overlap, or even how they might be further synthesized at some future date.

Implied Models of Man-in-Relationship: The Moral of Each

The first two perspectives, the humanistic-developmental theories (treated in Part I of this book) tend to be self-oriented or interpersonal, descriptive, normative, and small in scale. Actualization is the most humane, and in a sense tops off all the other theories by urging us to become true to ourselves as whole persons. Identity development views man through a lifetime of stages of personal development.

The second group of three perspectives, structure and change theories (Part II) covered the attempts of middle-range theorists to develop descriptive approaches and basic synthetic concepts to help unify many theories and forms of application. Group dynamics sees man as primarily influenced by his group memberships or images. Role bargaining is a way of reconciling society's conflicting role expectations for us. Interparty conflict as treated in these pages looks at the effects of opposition on mutual adjustment.

The third major group of three perspectives, behaviorist theories (Part III), treats the attempts of behaviorists to develop a more general theory. S-R behaviorism sees man as directly responding to his environment in a determined manner. Exchange focuses on the balance sheet of giving and receiving. Game theory zeroes in on the economics of interdependent payoffs.

The fourth group of four perspectives, congruency theories (Part IV), elaborates on the theme of congruence between persons as well as between a single person's ideas, feelings, and behavior. Cognitive dissonance views man as a consonance seeker. Symmetry focuses on the other person in a relationship as an attitude influencer. Interpersonal congruence tends to see man as a being who acts on the basis of his perceptions of himself and his view of how others label him. Self-consistency makes use of a counselor as a looking glass.

The fifth group of four perspectives, social interaction theories, (Part V), mainly treats the relationship between self and society, language, definitions of the situation and the basis of the social order from a comparatively micro-level perspective. Symbolic interactionism takes a broader view of man responding to others by taking their roles and engaging in self-conscious action. Labeling emphasizes the fact that continuing social pressure is a powerful motivation for changing one's self-concept. Dramaturgy sees man as basically a con artist. Ethnomethodology looks for the basis of the social order in conversational dialogue.

Each perspective and each group of perspectives has its ounce of truth to add to our knowledge of man in relationship. The student who masters them all will have many tools to give insight and scope to his understanding of people. Hopefully some day, some theoretician will be able to blend them all into a more comprehensive picture of society. Meanwhile, each individual student of societies must work with these fragmentary principles to spin out their own philosophy of life. Until each person takes up this task, we are all lesser human beings because of it. As I have said many times in the preceeding pages, when one of us fails to achieve self-actualization, we are all responsible. And we are all the lesser for it. Without a separate and collective achievement of self-actualization of all the members of our society, our society fails to reach its fullness. And conversely, without social actualization, self-actualization is impossible.

APPENDIX

A. Format Sheets
B. Recommended Reading and Study Questions
C. Classroom Simulation Games
D. Comparative Rating of the Sixteen Perspectives
E. Journal Guidelines and Format
   BIBLIOGRAPHY
   REFERENCES
   ALTERNATE TABLE OF CONTENTS

Appendix A

Format Sheets

As an aid to synthesizing the suggested readings and relating them to the chapters of this handbook, we present two different kinds of format report sheets. They provide a pedagogical procedure that should be helpful to those who read the handbook in conjunction with any form of reader or anthology.

MAIN TEXT READING REPORT

Your name: _____. Chap. # & Title: _____

Author of Your Text: _____. Today's date: _____. Class hour: _____

Please type or print your comments below (in dark-colored ink).

1. What was the general idea of the chapter? _____

   _____

2. What were the *three main points* of the chapter? (Preferably state your points as sociological (cause-effect) *hypotheses*. But at least try to bring out the soc. *concepts*._____

   _____

   _____

3. *Cite original author* of article or points, then the *editor* or author of the whole book, plus *page numbers* of one of the "corresponding chapters or articles" in your supplementary (more concrete) readings which you could use to *illustrate* some of the ideas discussed in the above chapter (as noted in I & II above)._____

   _____

   _____

4. Briefly show how the case material or data from your chosen supplementary reading illustrates your above-stated three points.

   _____

   _____

5. What was your opinion of the chapter and the illustrative article? What did you learn? _____

   _____

Use the back side of this page to continue any of your answers, if necessary.

6. Also on the back side of this page, type or print out *two* (or more) *discussion or debate questions* stimulated by or related to the topics of the above article(s) or chapter. Aim for questions which you think will stimulate provocative or controversial exchange of ideas between your fellow students. Be prepared to lead a small group discussion with your questions as a start.

N. B.: Turn in this completed page on the first class meeting of the week in which the above chapter(s) and readings were assigned.

   A fellow student may be asked to grade or at least share your statement orally with your group members or with the class as a whole.

SUPPLEMENTARY READING REPORT

Your name: _____. Chap. # & Title: _____

Original Author of article or chapter: _____

Editor of book, if any: _____. Today's date: _____.

Class hour: _____

Please type or print your comments below (in dark-colored ink).

1. What was the general idea of the article or chapter? _____

   _____

2. What were the *three main points* of the article or chapter? (Preferably state
   your points as sociological (cause-effect) *hypotheses*. But at least try to
   bring out the *sociological* concepts and implications.)

   _____

   _____

3. *Cite original author* and *page numbers* of the article or chapter, then the
   editor or author of the whole book (if any), for the *main text* on which you
   find *reference* to ideas related to your three main points stated above.

   _____

   _____

4. Briefly show how the ideas referred to in the *main text* are *illustrated*
   through aspects of the three main points noted above (in item II).

   _____

   _____

5. What was your opinion of the supplementary reading as well as the
   pertinent sections of the main text? What did you learn from these
   readings? _____

   _____

Use the back side of this page to continue any of your answers, if necessary.

6. Also on the back side of this page, type or print out *two* (or more)
   discussion or debate questions stimulated by or related to the topics of the
   above article(s) or chapter. Aim for questions which you think will
   stimulate provocative or controversial exchange of ideas between your
   fellow students. Be prepared to lead a small group discussion with your
   questions as a start.

**N. B.: Turn in this completed page on the first class meeting of the week in
which the above chapter(s) and readings were assigned.**

   A fellow student may be asked to grade or at least share your statement
orally with your group members or with the class as a whole.

Appendix B

Recommended Reading and Study Questions

PART I.
HUMANISTIC-DEVELOPMENTAL THEORIES

Reading for Social Actualization (Chapter 1)

The selection of Maslow which should be read ("A Theory of Human Motivation") represents some of the flavor of the humanistic school of social psychology with its use of parable and "warm" or emotional statement. Although this particular essay gives little in the way of empirical research, it does lay down a challenge to the reader and the social scientist, to aim high in selecting life goals. It nicely points toward the potentialities open to the fully human person in search of a better life.

The reading by Wheelis ("The Illusionless Man and the Visionary Maid") is a paradoxical one written by a novelist with a gift for humorously expressing the contradiction between the super-idealist and the super-realistic, between male and female. It has much of the flavor of the "theater of the absurd"—an attempt to find the meaningful in the many senseless contradictions of everyday life. The self-actualized person is somewhere in between, but probably closer to the idealist. The reading also suggests to us the difficulty of achieving a deep relationship or social actualization between two or more people or two parties who have opposite values in life.

Recommended Reading for Chapter 1
Social Actualization

Maslow, Abraham H. "A Theory of Human Motivation." *Psychological Review* 50, July 1943; 370–396. Bobbs-Merrill reprint P–509.

Maslow, Abraham. "The Jonah Complex." In W. Bennis, et al., *Interpersonal Dynamics*, 1968; 714–719.

Rogers, Carl. "A Theory of Personality and Behavior." Excerpted from *Client-Centered Therapy*, 1951; 483–524. Edited by W. S. Sahakian. Also in *The Psychology of Personality*, 1965; 475–493.

Rogers, Carl. "The Process of the Basic Encounter Group." Chapter 28 in J. F. T. Bugental, ed., *Challenges of Humanistic Psychology*, 1967; 261–276.

Wheelis, Allen B. "The Illusionless Man and the Visionary Maid." In W. Bennis, et al., *Interpersonal Dynamics*, 1968; 163–181. From *The Illusionless Man: Some Fantasies and Meditations on Disillusionment*, 1966.

Study Questions Overall

In light of the depth of most of these questions for all the theories, the discussion leader or instructor may find it helpful to break them down into a series of more concrete questions in "funnel" fashion, starting from the most general and introductory ones and running to the more specific and practical action issues.

Study Questions for Chapter 1
Social Actualization

1. Debate: Self-realization is the chief end of civilized man.
2. Discuss: Play is said by some writers to open the door to innovation and creativeness.
3. Does self-actualization precede social actualization? How so?
4. What kinds of people are more likely to achieve self-actualization?
5. Does anyone ever achieve full self-actualization?
6. For what kinds of people is self-actualization impossible?
7. What is the relation of peak experience to self-actualization?
8. Is there a middle-class bias in Maslow's meta-values?

9. What kind of person is most likely to profit from encounter group experiences? Least likely?

10. What are the qualities and competencies necessary to be a good encounter group leader?

11. Is simultaneous and interdependent self-actualization possible between two people? Is it likely?

12. What are some implications of this perspective when applied to groups, collectivities, and societies (primitive or industrialized), rather than just to individuals?

13. Are the concepts of this perspective devoid of social context?

14. Should a person be concerned about achieving self-actualization when the world is so full of social problems, and people are starving to death?

15. How do the advocates of this perspective attempt to reconcile the differences between empirical research and the realities and fullness of real life?

16. Do you believe that the recent history of contemporary American society dictates that we should put less stress on self-actualization and more on social actualization?

17. How is it possible to reconcile an industrialized and bureaucratized society with the ultimate needs and goals of the best in man?

18. To what extent are you personally self-actualized? Give some examples to show that you are, or have been at certain moments.

19. What traits in your personality or factors in your life situation might possibly prevent you from achieving self-actualization?

20. What might prevent you from achieving social actualization?

Reading for Identity Development (Chapter 2)

The reading of Elkind gives a very clear explanation of the perspective of Erikson. This perspective is neo-Freudian in that it contains the essentials of Freud's exploration of the unconscious and the structure of personality. These two perspectives of Freud and Erikson are useful for psychoanalytic purposes and were, in fact, developed by practical analysts. It is the author's opinion that Erikson's interpretation is closer to a coherent theory, hence the inclusion in this text. It contains the basis for a theory about the whole lifetime of a person, from birth to old age. This would be in effect a theory of socialization, or the development of the person. The student is urged to try to see the other fifteen theories of this text in the context of one or more of the eight stages of identity development.

Recommended Reading for Chapter 2
Identity Development

Brim, Orville G., Jr. "Family Structure and Sex Role Learning by Children: A Further Analysis of Helen Koch's Data." Chapter 50 in C. Backman and P. Secord, eds., *Problems in Social Psychology*, 1966; 431–440.

Elkind, David. "Erikson's Eight Ages of Man." *The New York Times Magazine*, April 5, 1970.

Erikson, Erik H. "The Problem of Ego Identity." *American Psychoanalytic Association Journal* 4, 1956; 56–121. Bobbs-Merrill reprint P–438. Reprinted in M. Stein, A. J. Vidich, and D. White, eds., *Identity and Anxiety*, 1960; 37–88.

Maccoby, Eleanor. "The Development of Moral Values and Behavior in Childhood." In J. A. Clausen, ed., *Socialization and Society*, 1968; 229–240.

McClelland, David C. "Some Themes in the Culture of India." In Henry Clay Lindgren, ed., *Contemporary Research in Social Psychology: A Book of Readings*, second edition, 1973; 197–235. Reprinted from A. R. Desai, ed., *Essays on Modernization of Underdeveloped Societies*, vol. 2. Department of Sociology, University of Bombay, 1972.

Study Questions for Chapter 2
Identity Development

1. What effect on one's social personality does one's relationship to parents (or significant others) have?

2. Are there distinct critical life problems existing at different periods of human life?

3. Are there stages of moral development? What might they be? By what mechanisms might they be developed?

4. What mechanisms (if any) are put forth by the socialization school of thought by which one advances across the stages of development?

5. How well must one master the developmental problems of one stage before advancing to the next?

6. How much do these critical issues depend on one's culture? On one's early childhood training? On heredity?

7. Does Erikson's treatment of the eight stages of man explain the process by which a person advances from one stage to the next? Or does he merely focus on the description of manifestations at the several stages of development?

8. What is likely to happen to the development of a young person who is intellectually and academically years ahead of his age group (say a 15-year-old entering college)?

9. In terms of this theory, what is likely to happen to a mentally retarded or "culturally deprived" child as far as his social development and relation to peers (or his own age group) is concerned?

10. What qualities of the relationship between socializer and socializee will affect the quality and extent of the effect or influence of socialization practices?

11. Is it reasonable to speak of the socialization of adults? Or of professional socialization? How would these differ in their emphasis from child socialization?

12. Are there actual (operationally observable) stages of human development, or are these merely hypothetical constructs?

13. How does Erikson's perspective depend on Freud's model of man (considering the unconscious: the id, ego, superego; substitution; sublimation; oral, anal, genital stages of child development, etc.)?

14. How do you believe the concepts of morality develop in people?

15. Compare the "typical" life cycles of men and women in America.

16. Do the same for men (or women) in two different societies.

PART II. STRUCTURE AND CHANGE THEORIES

Reading for Group Dynamics (Chapter 3)

The reading by Cartwright shows how a researcher on group dynamics has attempted to develop a theory and a research program on how to change people.

The reading from Schein is a fascinating attempt to state the essentials of any analysis of the process of changing people, in or out of the laboratory, prison, school or family.

Recommended Reading for Chapter 3
Group Dynamics

Unit A: The Primary Group

Cooley, Charles Horton. "Primary Groups." In A. P. Hare, E. Borgatta, and R. F. Bales, eds., *Small Groups*, 1955; 15–20.

Cooley, Charles Horton. "Primary Group and Human Nature." From *Social Organization*, 1909; 26–31. Reprinted in J. Manis and B. Meltzer, eds., *Symbolic Interaction*, 1972; 158–160.

Shils, Edward A. "The Study of the Primary Group." From Daniel Lerner and Harold Lasswell, eds., *The Policy Sciences*, 1951; 44–69. Also in Bobbs-Merrill reprint S–262.

Unit B: Reference Groups

Shibutani, Tamotsu, "Reference Groups as Perspectives." *American Journal of Sociology* 60, May 1955; 562–569. Reprinted in J. Manis and B. Meltzer, eds., *Symbolic Interaction*, 1972; 160–171. Bobbs-Merrill reprint S-259. Revised version in A. Rose, eds.: *Human Behavior and Social Processes*, 1962; 128–147.

Unit C: Group Dynamics

Bales, Robert F., "A Set of Categories for the Analysis of Small Group Interaction." *American Sociological Review*, 1950; 257–263. Bobbs-Merrill reprint S–5.

Cartwright, Dorwin, "Achieving Change in People: Some Applications of Group Dynamics Theory." *Human Relations* 4, 1951; 381–392. Reprinted in E. P. Hollander and R. G. Hunt, eds., *Current Perspectives in Social Psychology*, first edition, 1963; 506–516. Bobbs-Merrill reprint S–5.

Raven, Bertram H., and John R. P. French, Jr. "Legitimate Power, Coercive Power, and Observability in Social Influence." *Sociometry* 21, 1958; 83–97. Reprinted in C. Backman and P. Secord, eds., *Problems in Social Psychology*, 1966; 202–210.

Schachter, Stanley, "Deviation, Rejection, and Communication." *Journal of Abnormal and Social Psychology* 46, 1951; 190–207.

Reprinted in D. Cartwright and A. Zander, eds., *Group Dynamics*, second edition, 1960; 260–283; third edition, 1971; 165–181. Bobbs-Merrill reprint S–247.

Schein, Edgar H., "The Mechanisms of Change," in W. Bennis et al., *The Planning of Change*, 1969; 98–107.

Study Questions for Chapter 3
Group Dynamics

1. Distinguish between: a) membership vs. nonmembership reference groups; b) normative vs. comparative reference groups; c) positive vs. negative reference groups; d) primary vs. secondary groups.

2. Which side or polar type among each of the above four types or group dimensions is likely to have the strongest and most long lasting influence on a person's behavior?

3. Is a primary group necessarily also a reference group?

4. When does a group of which one is not a member have its strongest influence on one's behavior?

5. Why do people compare themselves to others?

6. What positive and negative effects can this comparison of oneself to others have?

7. When are groups more influential than individuals in changing a person's behavior?

8. Among three types of influence, which is likely to be most effective a) now, and b) in the long run? The three types of influence are a) identification, b) persuasion, and c) force. Why is your choice likely to be more effective than the others?

9. Why might a group of which one is a member have stronger influence on one's behavior than influence attempts by separate individuals?

10. Which kinds of leadership or authority relations make for a) a more productive group, b) a therapeutically more effective group? Choose among the following three types of authority: a) democratic; b) laissez faire; or c) autocratic-authoritarian.

11. What kind of social or emotional problems might best be treated by a group rather than by individual therapy? By client-centered vs. directive counseling?

12.   What are the conditions under which a primary group would have no effect on changing (or maintaining) a person's values—i.e., where no primary groups exist regarding some central life interest (e.g., surfing, meditating, being a monk or hermit, etc.)?

13.   Conformity appears to be a major theme in social psychology. Looking at the basic principles in social psychology, which research or perspectives indicate that man is a conformist? Are there any which suggest he is not?

14.   Demonstrate some hypotheses of group dynamics by playing a classroom simulation (or life experience) game (such as *Star Power*, by R. Garry Shirts).

15.   In what senses do animals belong to groups? Do they have reference groups?

16.   Trace the possible influence of an occupation (or an occupational ideology) upon its members as they rise in status within it.

Reading for Role Bargaining (Chapter 4)

The reading by Goode is the most basic theoretical statement available for this perspective. Although there seems to be no major group doing empirical research using this theory, Goode clearly points the way to those interested in developing this powerful theoretical perspective.

Recommended Reading for Chapter 4
Role Bargaining

Goode, William J., "A Theory of Role Strain." *American Sociological Review* 25, 1960; 483–496. Reprinted in C. Backman and P. Secord, eds., *Problems in Social Psychology*, 1966; 372–382. Bobbs-Merrill reprint S–402.

Study Questions for Chapter 4
Role Bargaining

1.   What is a role?

2.   Why is this concept so central to social science?

3.   What is role playing or role enactment?

4. What is "playing at a role" (or play acting)?

5. What is role taking (or empathy)?

6. What is role-making? How does it differ from conforming to a role expectation?

7. How does the concept of role differ or relate to status, norms, patterns of behavior, or mere expected behavior?

8. Can a person enact more than one role at a time? How so, or how not?

9. If a person must fulfill more than one role obligation over a period of time, are these role obligations not likely to come into conflict with one another?

10. How does one go about resolving such role conflict or strain between role obligations?

11. How or on what basis of priorities does one select from among the various required, expected, and possible roles he may or must fulfill?

12. What will cause a person to bargain with his roles in such a way as to form a new pattern of behavior, perhaps reflecting a newly arranged hierarchy of valued roles?

13. See last paragraphs of Goode's article for further questions.

14. How is role bargaining as a model useful in explaining patterns or types of behavior of persons or of collectivities or of aggregates or of groups?

15. Does the role bargaining model have greater potential for explaining or describing patterns of social behavior than other more atomistic cognitive models? Explain with an example. Why or why not?

16. How would you use role strain to explain the development of a delinquent career (such as that of hard drug user, car theft, membership in a criminal, conflict, violent, or retreatist gang or subculture, female delinquency, property delinquency or vandalism)?

17. How would you explain "good" or conforming behavior, using the role bargaining model?

18. Discuss the role requirements of some occupational or professional position, such as that of a minister or the minister's wife.

19. Trace the rise of a public hero and his fall from public favor.

Reading for Interparty Conflict (Chapter 5)

The reading from Deutsch shows how studies of conflict (as well as group dynamics) and other types of laboratory research can be made applicable and generalizable to the study of larger issues such as war and relations between nations. In short, Deutsch presents some very excellent and provocative ideas on how academic research can be made more relevant.

The second reading, by Milgram, looks at one of these larger issues. How would you go about describing a city? What characteristics would you look for? What is the relation of the density of population to the types of people living there, to the overload of information, to traditions and norms of behavior, especially concerning social involvement? Travelers will discover here some ways of looking more objectively at the atmosphere of different cities as seen by natives and foreign visitors. The reader should note the possibilities for analyzing the greater conflict that almost inevitably results from living in crowded quarters. In these circumstances we can see that greater knowledge (or bombardment with stimuli) frequently does not promote positive functions for the citizens or visitors. Quite probably in competitive Western societies the knowledge becomes information overload and leads to greater conflict or opposition and aggression of people toward one another.

Although these readings do not focus intrinsically on the positive functions of conflict (which Simmel observed), they do present very real issues of potential conflict which we need to solve in our everyday lives. Our very real tasks are first to empathically learn about and secondly to bargain integratively with our fellow men in order to turn our conflicts with him into positive ends. At very least, these two readings touch upon a conflict between social scientific knowledge and practical affairs. They point indirectly to a resolution through an open-minded attempt to generalize and synthesize in a kind of dialectical movement of ideas from life to laboratory and back again to life.

Recommended Reading for Chapter 5
Interparty Conflict

Angell, Robert. "The Sociology of Human Conflict." In E. McNeil, ed., *The Nature of Human Conflict*, 91–115.

Deutsch, Morton. "Socially Relevant Science: Reflections on Some Studies of Interpersonal Conflict." *American Psychologist* 24:12, December 1969; 1076–1092.

Milgram, Stanley. "The Experience of Living in Cities." In Alvin M. Snadowsky, ed., *Social Psychology Research: Laboratory-Field Relationships,* 1972; 272–296. From *Science,* 1970, 1967; 1461–1468.

Sartori, Giovanni. "Politics, Ideology, and Belief Systems." In Leigh Marlowe, ed., *Basic Topics in Social Psychology: An Interdisciplinary and Intercultural Reader,* 1972; 433–452. Reprinted from the *American Political Science Review,* 63: 2, 1969.

Schermerhorn, R. A. "The Polish American." In *These Our People: Minorities in American Culture,* 1949; 265–290. Abridged in Yehudi A. Cohen, ed., *Social Structure and Personality,* 1961; 407–420.

Simmel, Georg. "The Triad." Chapter 4 in K. Wolff, ed. *The Sociology of Georg Simmel,* 1950; 145–169.

Naess, Arne. "A Systematization of Gandhian Ethics of Conflict Resolution." *Journal of Conflict Resolution* 2, 1958; 140–155.

Study Questions for Chapter 5
Interparty Conflict

1. Is conflict between persons and groups (and between persons, collectivities or ethnic groups) inevitable?

2. Is it always harmful?

3. When does conflict serve useful functions?

4. How does value conflict differ from interest conflict? Which type has the most far-reaching effects?

5. Which type has the most positive effects on the relationship between the two or more parties involved? Which type has the most negative effects on the relationship?

6. Under what conditions is conflict most intense?

7. What are some of the forms of conflict?

8. What are some of the forms of conflict resolution?

9. Is integrative bargaining possible in the face of a zero-sum game?

10. Is distributive bargaining possible in a nonzero sum game?

11. Does this mean that it is easier to, or more common to bargain distributively in all of our interparty conflicts?

12. How do various degrees and kinds of communication between parties affect the length, seriousness, and outcome of their struggle?

13. What effects does the depth of the relationship have on the forms, intensity and possible outcomes of a conflict?

14. How much knowledge of the other party is helpful to achieving smooth coordination of actions and deeper levels of sharing in the face of conflict?

15. Discuss the dating and courting process in terms of crisis, ritual, stages, and turning points in development.

PART III. BEHAVIORIST THEORIES

Reading for Stimulus-Response Behaviorism (Chapter 6)

The article by Bandura, Ross, and Ross is an excellent example of empirical laboratory research in the S-R tradition applied to social behavior. It deals in general with roles, motivation, and attitude change. In particular it examines the conditions for imitation of role models by children. Quantitative data was gathered based on the experimenter's direct observation of the subjects' behavior. The explicit treatment of secondary reinforcement and imitation makes this study definitely social rather than merely individual psychological research.

Recommended Reading for Chapter 6
Stimulus-Response Behaviorism

Bandura, Albert, D. Ross, and S. Ross. "A Comparative Test of the Status Envy, Social Power, and Secondary Reinforcement Theories of Identificatory Learning." *Journal of Abnormal and Social Psychology* 67, 1963; 527–534. Reprinted in C. Backman and P. Secord, eds., *Problems in Social Psychology*, 1966; 440–447.

Skinner, B. F. "Operant Behavior: Social and Verbal Behavior." In William S. Sahakian, ed., *Social Psychology, Experimentation Theory, Research*, and *International and Human Behavior* by B. F. Skinner, 1953; 297–312.

Study Questions for Chapter 6
Stimulus-Response Behaviorism

1. What is the pleasure principle? Hedonism?

2. Do men always respond to stimuli?

3. When don't they respond?

4. When do they respond alike or in patterns?

5. How do we come to associate secondary stimuli with a desired reward in such a way that we respond to the associated stimulus even in the absence of the original primary stimulus?

6. What is classical conditioning?

7. What is operant conditioning?

8. Is reward and/or punishment for a completed act more effective in stamping in or stamping out a behavior pattern than merely associating a secondary stimulus with a reward?

9. What is the black box model of personality (or of group behavior)?

10. How does S-R apply to complex social behavior, involving reflective thought? Comparatively how well does it apply relative to other social psychological perspectives?

11. How might a person's definition of a situation (or definition of stimuli, usually involving selective perception) affect his response to the stimuli?

12. Which is more important in predicting behavior of a person—knowledge of all possible operating stimuli, or knowledge of his definition of his situation at the crucial moment in time just before his action or response?

13. What is imitation?

14. What is secondary reinforcement?

15. What is extinction?

16. What basic S-R principles can be used to change the behavior of a person?

17. How would you apply the S-R model to counseling of antisocial children?

18. What limits would this perspective have in dealing with people (rather than lower animals)?

19. Evaluate the effects upon personality development of harsh or physical punishment versus love-oriented child rearing techniques.

20. Why does the law declare that it is impossible for a child below a certain age to commit a crime?

22. Criticize the shortcomings of the distinction between derived and basic needs.

23. Under what circumstances should an attempt be made to suppress deviant groups by police action?

24. Discuss the utility of the prison system for reforming criminals.

Reading for Exchange Theory (Chapter 7)

The reading from Michal McCall looks at the history of courtship practices for insights into the social exchange that occurs between potential marriage partners. She suggests that the change from the traditional or institutionalized permanent marriage agreement has changed. We can now gain greater insight into the presently more acceptable customs of divorce and remarriage if we see that even married persons remain more or less permanently available for additional marriage alliances. Thus, we have a most interesting theoretical application of exchange theory.

Recommended Reading for Chapter 7
Exchange Theory

Homans, George C. "Social Behavior as Exchange." *American Journal of Sociology* 63, May 1958; 597–606. Reprinted in Hollander and Hunt, eds., *Current Perspectives in Social Psychology*, 1963; 436–446. Reprinted in W. Bennis et al., *Interpersonal Dynamics*, second edition, 1968; 523–539. Bobbs-Merrill reprint S–122.

McCall, Michal. "Courtship as Social Exchange." In B. Farber, ed., *Kinship and Family Organization*, 1966; 190–200.

Study Questions for Chapter 7
Exchange Theory

1. Do people usually expect a reward for their actions?

2. If I give something to a person, am I likely to expect a return for the favor?

3. Under what conditions? In what form?

4. Suppose my gift is purely my affection, with no monetary value. What kind of return, if any, am I likely to expect?

5. What is likely to happen if I do not receive a reward or a return for my gifts?

6. Suppose I give something of moderate or small intrinsic value to another person at great cost to myself. Am I then likely to look for a return greater than the intrinsic value of the gift? Why or why not?

7. When does the norm of reciprocity cease to operate? Is it a universal norm? Is there a norm that is more universal?

8. Why is the refusal of communication (solitary confinement) considered one of the most severe forms of punishment?

9. Discuss the potlatch.

10. Under what conditions does profit cease to be a motive for or a predictor of human behavior?

11. Does the profit motive have less application to social behavior than to nonsocial behavior of individuals or groups?

12. Is this the most parsimonious and universally applicable social principle (i.e., the exchange principle)?

13. How well does exchange theory account for the individual perceptions of rewards and costs in social situations? In nonsocial situations?

14. How could you apply the exchange theory to try to change a person's behavior in a given situation?

15. Does exchange have an advantage over S-R (say, the Skinnerian version of) behaviorism for controlling human behavior?

16. Why is gambling so widespread? Is it an instinctive activity?

Reading for Game Theory (Chapter 8)

Rapoport's article explains the basic theory quite fully, together with many interesting special cases. The reader should recall that Deutsch, in the earlier article, Chapter 5 of this book, makes a case in part for the value of game theory and similar laboratory approaches when they applied to real-life situations.

Recommended Reading for Chapter 8
Game Theory

Rapoport, Anatol. "Game Theory and Human Conflict." Chapter 10 in
   Elton B. McNeil, ed., *The Nature of Human Conflict*, 1965;
   195–226. Reprinted in E. Borgatta, ed., *Social Psychology*;
   559–579.

Study Questions for Chapter 8
Game Theory

1. Is life a game? In what sense?

2. How does game playing differ from real life?

3. What are the components of games?

4. When does play become a game?

5. Is winning always the object of a game? For what kinds of people
    or under what conditions would winning not be the object?

6. How important are rules to game playing?

7. Are games merely social exercises or pastimes?

8. How does a game differ from a (life) script?

9. What are some of the latent functions of game playing?

10. What are some of the latent dysfunctions of game playing?

11. Is game theory really a method or procedure rather than a theory?

12. Is it easy to decide what are the possible inputs vs. outputs, costs
    vs. rewards of a series of actions between two parties in a
    relationship?

13. How can you incorporate individual (players') values and
    perceptions into the game theory matrix or model of human
    social behavior?

14. Are most real life games zero-sum games (where what one party
    gains the other loses)?

15. Is the prisoner's dilemma a zero-sum game?

16. Set up a game theoretical matrix for high vs. low teacher
    standards and high vs. low students effort in a course. Give
    reasons for assigning the relative weights (gain or loss outcomes)
    to each cell.

17. Under what circumstances are deviant groups tolerated or
    suppressed?

PART IV. CONGRUENCY THEORIES

Reading for Cognitive Dissonance (Chapter 9)

Many of the aspects of cognitive dissonance are illustrated in the Cohen and Brehm article which is an experimental report treating the hypothesis that: *As the pressure to make a choice increases, the magnitude of postchoice dissonance and consequent reevaluation of alternatives decreases.* Cohen and Brehm attempt to control variables in a kind of laboratory situation with paper and pencil measures. The subjects are individual fraternity pledges. There follows a postscript which is a brief and thoughtful discussion of the determinants of dissonance in experimental settings.

Recommended Reading for Chapter 9
Cognitive Dissonance

Cohen, Arthur R., and Jack W. Brehm. "An Experiment in Illegitimate Coercion, Volition, and Attitude Change." Reprinted from *Explorations in Cognitive Dissonance*, 1962. Reprinted in Carl Backman and Paul Secord, eds., *Problems in Social Psychology: Selected Readings*, 1966; 113–115.

Festinger, Leon. "Theory of Cognitive Dissonance." From William S. Sahakian, ed., *Social Psychology; Experimentation, Theory, Research*, 1972; 254–257. Reprinted from Leon Festinger, *A Theory of Cognitive Dissonance*, 1957.

Study Questions for Chapter 9
Cognitive Dissonance

1. How do you handle contradictory bits of knowledge in both concrete and abstract terms?

2. What causes, conditions, or situations often lead to such contradictory ideas?

3. What kind of turning points or decisions lead to, or result from, dissonant cognitions?

4. How would you use the principles of this perspective to change a concrete person or a group you are familiar with?

5. When might dissonant ideas be a) desirable, b) useful, c) necessary, or d) pleasant?

6. How strong must the dissonance be before it has any effect on one's thought or behavior?

7. How strong must be the dissonance before it becomes intolerable?

8. When might resolution of dissonance confirm a behavior pattern?

9. Is man a conformist?

10. Is the primary emphasis of this theory on cognition or behavior? How so?

Reading for Symmetry (Chapter 10)

The article by Levinger and Breedlove uses a survey approach to study social perceptions and self-perception. In particular, it reports evidence on actual agreement, assumed agreement (on marriage goals), and marital satisfaction of husbands and wives. The article is a clear example of research done in the tradition of Newcomb's AB-X model known as the symmetry perspective.

Recommended Reading for Chapter 10
Symmetry

Levinger, George, and James Breedlove, "Interpersonal Attraction," from Michael A. Malec, ed., *Attitude Change*, 1971. Reprinted from George Levinger and James Breedlove, "Interpersonal Attraction and Agreement: A Study of Marriage Partners." *Journal of Personality and Social Psychology* 3, 1966; 367–372.

Newcomb, Theodore. "The Prediction of Interpersonal Attraction," *American Psychologist* 1, 1956; 575–586. Reprinted in E. Borgatta, ed., *Social Psychology*, 1969; 464–484. Reprinted in C. Backman and P. Secord, eds., *Problems in Social Psychology*; 168–179. Bobbs-Merrill reprint S–209.

Study Questions for Chapter 10
Symmetry

1. If you have a close friend who likes avant-garde films, how are you likely to feel about such films?

2. What if you had no previous knowledge about such films?

3. What if you previously disliked such films, and now your close friend invites you to see such a movie with him (or her)? What would you do?

4. In what ways could you possibly handle such a situation?

5. What effects might it have on your relationship or your cinematic interest?

6. Suppose you and a newfound acquaintance are both avid sports enthusiasts. How is this likely to make you feel towards that new acquaintance?

7. What if your common interest is in promoting social betterment? What is likely to result for your relationship and for the people who might be helped?

8. What if your common interest is in finding a marriage partner? And you are mutually eligible?

9. Suppose you and a close friend of the same sex are both seriously interested in the same other eligible person of the opposite sex? What will happen to your liking for one another (i.e., you and your same-sex friend)?

10. What are you and your close friend of the same sex likely to communicate to one another, if anything?

11. What is the general effect of differing strengths of attitude to the object and feeling toward one another?

12. Under what conditions is (balance or) symmetry unlikely to result from an AB-X situation?

13. What if you have a well-liked pet chicken, and the chicken likes chicken feed? Are you likely to change your mind about eating chicken feed?

14. How could you as a salesperson or persuader use the symmetry perspective to sell some object to a customer or client? Say you are selling something like apples, flowers, raffle tickets, computer services, Fords, airplanes, deodorant, etc.

Reading for Interpersonal Congruence (Chapter 11)

The selection by Backman, Secord, and Pierce is a clear example of a survey-type approach to studying self- and social perception, consensus, and attitude change in a classroom setting. But the manipulation of variables is typical of a laboratory setting. In any case, the reader should try to carefully pick out the three key elements of the perspective and the possible modes of resolution in order to see the applicability of the theory, per se. An especially crucial point of this research for the theme of this text is that the research is guided explicitly by a theory.

Recommended Reading for Chapter 11
Interpersonal Congruence

Backman, Carl W., Paul F. Secord, and Jerry Pierce. "Resistance to Change in the Self-Concept as a Function of Consensus Among Significant Others." pp. 462–467 in C. Backman and P. Secord, eds., *Problems in Social Psychology*. Reprinted from "Resistance to Change in the Self-Concept as a Function of Perceived Consensus Among Significant Others," *Sociometry* 26, 1963; 102–111.

Secord, Paul F., and Carl W. Backman. "Personality Theory and the Problem of Stability and Change in Individual Behavior: An Interpersonal Approach." *Psychological Review* 68, 1961; 21–33. Reprinted in E. P. Hollander and R. G. Hunt, eds., *Current Perspectives in Social Psychology*, first and second edition.

Study Questions for Chapter 11
Interpersonal Congruence

1. What advance does this perspective make over self-consistency, cognitive dissonance, or symmetry?

2. In what sense is this an interdisciplinary perspective?

3. How does it explain both stability and change in interpersonal interaction?

4. Does the explicitness of the matrix permit the perspective to be more effective on the four characteristics of a good theory, namely, explanatory power, information value, predictability and testability or ease of application? How so?

5. Is it a more synthetic theory than others? Is it broader in scope of application?

6. How does it interrelate self and other, or the psychological and sociological aspects of human social behavior?

7. How important are one's perceptions to his behavior toward others?

8. On specific issues at a given period of time, are individuals more likely to achieve congruency than incongruency among the three components of the matrix?

Reading for Self-Consistency (Chapter 12)

The very brief selection from Lecky's work provides an overview and a taste of his ideas in his own words. It discusses personal sensitivities and emotions as related to the definition a person gives to himself.

Recommended Reading for Chapter 12
Self-Consistency

Lecky, Prescott, "The Theory of Self-Consistency." In C. Gordon and M. Gergen, eds., *The Self in Social Interaction*, 1968; 297–298. Excerpted from Prescott Lecky, *Self-Consistency: A Theory of Personality*, 1945; Appendix III.

Study Questions for Chapter 12
Self-Consistency

1. How does the degree of centrality of a person's life interests affect his actions?

2. How does this centrality of interest in something or someone affect his behavior toward that thing or person?

3. How would you characterize the configuration of interests and social personality traits of a person you know? Consider the strength of these central concerns especially as they affect his behavior in problematic situations.

4. How would you use this characterization to point up potentially harmful inconsistencies in someone's personality?

5. As a counselor, how might you use these configurations of a person's self-concept or personality? Suppose, for example, that:
   a. a student has a reading problem and wants to go to college?
   b. a student has a mathematics problem in high school and wants to be an engineer?
   c. a student wants to be a pilot but cannot afford lessons?
   d. a student wants a higher degree, has good mechanical skills, but experiences high emotional tension or strain with long hours of study?

6. How could you combine this perspective with cognitive dissonance and explain change in a person's self-concept over time?

Part V. SOCIAL INTERACTION THEORIES

Reading for Symbolic Interactionism (Chapter 13)

Meltzer does an excellent job of summarizing the essential points of George H. Mead's social psychology. It is most important for the beginning student to understand this unique and subtle explanation of interpersonal behavior. The apparent vagueness of the description seems to reflect the true state of present theoretical knowledge of social interaction. This, in turn, makes it difficult to do definitive quantitative research following the pragmatist tradition. Thus, theoretical elaboration perhaps related to case studies is more typical from scholars in this school. Hence, this theoretical reading was considered highly typical and appropriate because this text is aiming toward a summary, comparison, and potential synthesis of perspectives. Once again, symbolic interactionism is really a metatheory (i.e., a theory about theories), and is in general more abstract than the others.

Recommended Reading for Chapter 13
Symbolic Interactionism

Hulett, J. E., Jr. "A Symbolic Interactionist Model of Communication." Part I, *AV Communications Review*, Spring 1966.

Kuhn, Manford H., and Thomas S. McPartland. "An Empirical Investigation of Self-Attitudes." *American Sociological Review*, 19, February 1954; 68–76. Reprinted in J. Manis and B. Meltzer, eds., 120–133.

Meltzer, Bernad N. "Mead's Social Psychology." Chapter 1 in J. Manis and B. Meltzer, eds., *Symbolic Interaction*, first edition, 1967; 5-24. Manis and Meltzer, 2nd ed., 1972; 4–22 and 575–577. Excerpted in S. Spitzer, ed., *The Sociology of Personality*, 1969.

Shibutani, Tamotsu, and Kian M. Kwan. *Ethnic Stratification: A Comparative Approach*, 1965; 572–589.

Stryker, Sheldon, "Relationships of Married Offspring and Parent: A Test of Mead's Theory." *American Journal of Sociology* 62, 1956; 308–319. Revised version in A. Rose, ed., *Human Behavior and Social Processes*, entitled "Conditions of Accurate Role-Taking: A Test of Mead's Theory." Chapter 3; 41–62.

Study Questions for Chapter 13
Symbolic Interactionism

1. What is the self? What are the conditions under which it emerges?

2. How important is the self?

3. Distinguish between self-image and self-concept.

4. What is the importance of the "I-Me" interaction process?

5. In what ways is the self a social product?

6. Does fashion, as in clothes, promote freedom, autonomy, and choice, or does it regiment and confine taste and choice?

7. What is social consciousness? What are the conditions under which social consciousness emerges?

8. What is a symbol?

9. How does a symbol become a significant symbol?

10. Why is it important to understand the difference between a mere signal and a significant symbol (or a gesture)?

11. What is the difference between role-taking and role-making? Why is the distinction important in social research, and in social life in general?

12. What is the difference between role-taking and empathy? Of what importance is the distinction for understanding social relations?

13. Of what importance is the concept of the social act for observing and understanding the possibility of joint action between people?

14. What concepts distinguish man from the lower animals?

15. What is the distinction between the individual act and the reflective act?

16. What is the difference between the nonreflective and the reflective act?

17. What is the difference between a significant other, a reference group, and the generalized other?

18. What other social psychological perspectives are closely interrelated with symbolic interactionism? In what ways? Which theories are not related to symbolic interactionism?

19. How does Mead make the past, present, and future relevant to individual acts (and ultimately to social behavior)?

20. Is symbolic interactionism a theory, in the strict sense of the word? How so? If not, is it at least a frame of reference?

21. Is there any significance of this perspective bearing on social or political action in modern society?

22. Does society precede the self in time? In importance?

23. What classifications would you use to interpret the results of the Twenty Statements Tests (or the "Who am I?" test) given to students, professionals of a certain type, housewives, or people in general?

24. How useful is symbolic interactionism for generating vs. explaining research and theory in social psychology?

25. What are the limitations of symbolic interactionism?

26. Why is stimulus-response behaviorism in more favor among psychologists and symbolic interactionism so among sociologists? What does this tell us about the perspectives of these two disciplines as a whole?

Reading for Labeling (Chapter 14)

Probably the most explicit statement available of labeling hypotheses applied to a concrete case is the article by Thomas Scheff. His hypotheses are related only by impliction to the nine steps described above. The reader should be aware that "mental illness" is viewed by labeling theorists not as a pathology, but rather as a label for extreme behavior in response to extreme social pressures. The pressures may in turn result from or at least be related to, environmental difficulties and problems in the organization of the person's society or family or reference groups.

Recommended Reading for Chapter 14
Labeling

Becker, Howard S. "Becoming a Marijuana User." *American Journal of Sociology* 59, 1953; 242–255.

Reprinted in Jerome G. Manis and B. Meltzer, eds., *Symbolic Interaction*, 1967; 411–422. Reprinted in H. Becker, *The Outsiders*, 41–58. Reprinted in Bartlett Stoodley, ed., *Society and Self*, 297–308. Bobbs-Merrill reprint S–9.

Scheff, Thomas. "The Role of the Mentally Ill and the Dynamics of Mental Disorders: A Research Framework." *Sociometry* 26, December 1963; 436–453. Reprinted in S. Spitzer and N. Denzin, eds., *The Mental Patient*, 8–22. Reprinted in S. Dinitz, R. Dynes, and A. Clarke, *Deviance*, 1969; 505–515.

Smith, H. C. "Sensitivity to People." From the introduction of *Sensitivity to People*, 1959. Reprinted in Hans Toch and Henry Clay Smith, eds., *Social Perception*, 1968; 10–19.

Study Questions for Chapter 14
Labeling

1. Do you put people in pigeon holes?

2. Where? When? Why? Who do you do it to? With what results?

3. Do people put you in pigeon holes?

4. Which ones? Do they give you a nickname?

5. How does it make you feel?

6. Is there much basis in fact for their labeling of you?

7. What are some good effects of labeling or typing people?

8. Is it a necessary or useful device?

9. What are some possible negative effects of stereotyping?

10. Under what conditions does a person accept others' labels of himself?

11. When might he reject them?

12. Does the effect of the label increase when it is used publicly rather than privately (in the absence of third parties)?

13. How can you rationalize or "neutralize" a potentially unacceptable or negative label of your actions or your personality as a whole?

14. Under what conditions or in what situations might a person accept and then use a label given to him to justify or motivate his behavior?

15. How would you use labeling to change a person to your way of thinking?

16. How would you get another to act or behave differently?

17. What are the nine steps in the labeling process?

18. What kind of detail is necessary in order to easily apply this theory?

19. Is the theory better at describing or explaining reality or social processes? What is its information value vs. explanatory power?

20. Discuss some possible professional biases of lawyers, physicians, nurses, or engineers. Is there a "professional mentality?"

How great a difference is there in character according to region in America?

21. Under what circumstances should an attempt be made to suppress deviant groups by police action? What makes behavior criminal?

Reading for Dramaturgy (Chapter 15)

The recommended basic statement from Goffman defines and discusses certain types of secrets and discrepant roles with characteristic dramaturgical insights. Practically every dramaturgical study or insight is based in some way on these ideas.

Recommended Reading for Chapter 15
Dramaturgy

Goffman, Erving. "Discrepant Roles." Chapter 4 in *The Presentation of Self in Everyday Life*, 1959; 141–166.

Goffman, Erving. "The Moral Career of the Mental Patient," *Psychiatry* 22, 1959; 125–131. Reprinted in C. Backman and P. Secord eds., 455–461. Reprinted in G. Stone and H. Farberman, eds., *Social Psychology Through Symbolic Interaction*, 1970; 669–688.

Study Questions for Chapter 15
Dramaturgy

1. How valid is the model of the stage or theater in representing human social life?

2. What are the various kinds of roles people enact in everyday life?

3. Is it humanly possible to manage the impressions we give (or give off) to those we deal with?

4. What kind of person is better at this?

5. Is such a person necessarily less sincere or less spontaneous for engaging in such management of his image?

6. Are salesmen always insincere?

7. What kind of men make the best salesmen?

8. How would you distinguish between the formal and informal social systems, or the front and backstage regions of behavior?

9. Does the uniqueness of an actor's personality mean that no two actors can play the same role?

10. How can one enact a role and yet retain role distance (i.e., giving off signs of apartness or at least partial separation of one's real feelings from the present role situation)?

11. What are some kinds of discrepant roles (where the actor is playing for two audiences at once, though not necessarily visibly)?

12. What is meant by "working the system?"

13. How does the external appearance of a person affect the impression he leaves?

14. How can one discover or unmask the real other person when so many clever masks are available to all?

15. When is it not advisable to present ourselves in the best light? In a good light?

16. How would you go about writing objectively on a subject which you held strong biases?

Reading for Ethnomethodology (Chapter 16)

Alfred Schultz is probably the philosopher most cited by ethnomethodologists. Hence, his article is recommended here. Although Schultz does not use the documentary method, the beauty of his insights and clarity of his statements are most worthy of emulation. Such philosophical interpretations are the avowed goal of ethnomethodologists. In conclusion, it is clear that we as students of social psychology must take on many of the characteristics of "the stranger" in order to see more clearly beneath the surface of our relationships with our fellow man.

Recommended Reading for Chapter 16
Ethnomethodology

Garfinkel, Harold. "Common Sense Knowledge of Social Structures: The Documentary Method of Interpretation in Lay and Professional Fact Finding." Chapter 3 in *Studies in Ethnomethodology*, 76–103. Reprinted in J. Scher, ed., Theories of Mind.

Garfinkel, Harold. "Studies of the Routine Grounds of Everyday Activities." *Social Problems* 11:3, Winter 1964; 225–250. Reprinted in H. Garfinkel, *Studies in Ethnomethodology*, 35–75.

Schutz, Alfred. "The Stranger." In A. Schutz, ed., Collected Papers, vol. II, 1964; 91–105. Reprinted in M. Stein, A. Vidich and D. White, *Identity and Anxiety*, 1960; 98–109.

Study Questions for Chapter 16
Ethnomethodology

1. How is social order possible?

2. In the face of continual conflict between people, how is social order possible?

3. What are the underlying, usually hidden, rules that make it possible for two or more people to coordinate their action (or even to converse)?

4. How are these rules brought to the threshold of awareness?

5. Does breaking unconscious norms bring them to awareness? Why?

6. Why is it easier to analyze the operations of these underlying rules of social interaction by explicitly interpreting both sides of a two-person conversation (using the documentary method of interpretation)?

Appendix C

Classroom Simulation Games

A simulation game is a set of rules for a game to be played by the students to demonstrate some theoretical principles, as well as to help sensitize participants to their own feelings. Ideally, students should work in pairs to organize such games. When the game is completed, each of the students who helped organize it should take a separate perspective from among the sixteen and demonstrate step-by-step how the events of the game fit the concepts and hypotheses of the perspective. Instructions for many such games are currently available. One of the best compendiums is J. William Pfeiffer and John E. Jones, *A Handbook of Structured Experiences for Human Relations Training*, now in several volumes. Complete catalogs are also readily available. Since not all of the games are directly usable, some searching must be done for a game that shows change or commitment over time of persons or groups. One of the most fascinating of such games is known as *Star Power*. It was developed by R. Garry Shirts. Instructions are available for $3 from:

> Simile II
> 218 Twelfth Street
> P.O. Box 910
> Del Mar, CA 92014.

AGENDA FOR ANY SIMULATION GAME

I. *Preparation*

Choose an appropriate "group experience" or simulation game well in advance (at least a week before your planned presentation). Ask instructor for a list of references containing some (if you have no original ideas of your own).

    A. Write the names of the two (or three organizers/presenters of the demonstration on an 8-½ x 11 piece of paper. After the name of each person, state which one (or at most two) theory (-ies) that each organizer tentatively plans to use to analyze the demonstration. Each demonstrator should focus on one theory in his follow-up analysis. State the nature of your demonstration, together with the reference or complete source and page numbers. Note class hour and length of planned presentation on this page as well.

    B. Sign up on the instructor's agenda or schedule of orals at least a week ahead in order to avoid conflicts with other demonstrations or presentation of the theories themselves.

    C. Practice your game/experience and the debriefing session informally with friends before doing it in class. Develop an agenda at this time.

II. *The Experience Itself*

    A. Present instructions clearly.

        1. Base your presentation on your prepared minute-by-minute agenda for the whole oral demonstration and debriefing session.

    B. Make use of group process observers. (Do this especially with latecomers.)

        1. Appoint specific persons to look for instances of one theory each.

        2. OR: Have them make use of some variant of a group process observer report form (available from instructor). These observers will be expected to report their observations later to the class as a whole. Remind them of this when you assign them their tasks.

        3. Be absolutely certain that no one is left out of direct participation in some way. Otherwise, boredom will result, without fail.

III. *Debriefing Session*

This part of the demonstration is of crucial importance. Plan ahead to allow a good 15 to 20 minutes for this debriefing session after the simulation or demonstration proper. This time should be budgeted into your minute-by-minute written agenda as a guide.

    A.   Solicit the views of participants.

        1.   Behavior: Who did what to whom and why? Who said what with what significance?

        2.   Expression of feeling by participants: How did you feel when so-and-so said or did such-and-such to you (or to a third party, namely, to X)?

        3.   Ask participants what insights they gained into: motives, strategy, tactics, rules, and procedures; goals, group processes, group structure, social class behavior; leadership, followership, intentions, outcomes, unique characteristics of group members, etc.

    B.   Group process observers' report (based for example on the report sheet available from the instructor, or based on some similar check list).

IV.   *Step-by-step illustration* of your chosen single theory by you the organizer, and separately by your partner. This is the most crucial step in your oral demonstration. Spend a full five minutes per theory showing how it applies.

    A.   Write key concepts, hypotheses and diagram (if appropriate or traditional) on the chalk board before the application is described.

        1.   First state what was time 1 (before), the crucial intervening event, and then time 2 (after).

        2.   Who was the protagonist(s) in your demonstration (or reading)?

        3.   Summarize at the beginning and end of your presentation (like any good public speaker does).

    B.   This application should be addressed to those students who may not fully understand the theory you are illustrating. Be as explicit as possible. Avoid oversimplification or telescoping of the theory into a meaningless reference to a couple of related concepts. Cover all the points which would ordinarily go into a careful 50-word summary of each theory. And show how each point and each concept applies (at t_1 and t_2). Use carefully prepared notes for this part of your presentation.

V. *Wrap-Up*

    A.   Ask: What theories did participants themselves see operating in the course of the demonstration? What applications might this experience have to real life situations?

B. Pose two or three provocative questions, one at a time, for a five-minute follow-up discussion related either to your chosen theory or to the demonstration carried out.

C. Allow three minutes or so at the very end of class for possible student grading of your oral presentation. (The instructor will decide whether to do this. It will be based on forms developed by him for this purpose. You may however insist on this student grading if you prefer.)

If you prefer to do some other type of oral presentation, such as a debate, or a more individual report, ask instructor for a copy of instructions or suggestions, and a reading list. Original ideas are nearly always preferred, however.

Appendix D

Comparative Ratings of Sixteen Perspectives

	Explanatory Power	Information Value	Predictability	Testability	Ease of Application
Cognitive Dissonance	H	L	H	H	H
Labeling	M	M	L	L	H
Symmetry	M	L	H	H	H
Self-Consistency	M	M	M	M	H
Interpersonal Congruence	H	M	M	H	M
Role Bargaining	H	M	M	M	H
S-R	H	M	M	H	H
Exchange	H	M	H	H	H
Game	H	H	H	H	L
Symbolic Interaction	H	H	M	M	H
Socialization	L	H	L	L	M
Groups	M	M	L	H	H
Conflict	M	L	L	M	M
Dramaturgy	L	M	L	L	H
Ethnomethodology	L	L	L	L	M
Actualization	L	L	L	L	H
General Systems	H	L	H	L	M

Key: H = High; M = Medium; L = Low;

Appendix E

Journal Guidelines and Format

In consultation with the instructor a journal may be written in place of certain other tasks for the course. A journal requires the student to have good, regular study habits, though it has the possibility of stimulating more creative and immediately meaningful results. If you intend to choose this option you should draw up two copies of a written contract stating your intention to do so along with a list of other tasks for which you would like to be graded, or at least evaluated. The contract, in duplicate, should be submitted by the third week of classes. The following format is ideal, but need not be followed slavishly. If you do follow it however you will automatically cover all the essential points for the journal and for the course.

I. *Procedure*
    A. Submit the carefully and legibly written (or typed) journal in two parts (preferably in two booklets). The first installment must be submitted before the midterm exam. The second installment must be submitted on the last class day, or beforehand. The two major segments may be prepared in two separate booklets. An ideal arrangement for the teacher's eyes would be to type the points of your journal on loose-leaf pages.

II. *Content and Format*
    A. In the left column (or left page), note down reflections, summaries of events experienced or articles read that relate to the themes, topics, social issues and problems suggested by the readings of the course.
        1. The journal should be prepared by dividing it into two parallel columns. Or better yet, the booklet should

carefully distinguish the left side from the right side of any pair of open pages.

2. The left column (or left page) should record your observations and experiences, including biographical or autobiographical and contextual background.

3. Then in the left column (or left page, note down reflections, summaries of events experienced or articles read that relate to the themes, topics, social issues and problems suggested by the readings of the course.

4. The right hand side of the page (or the right page itself) should record your very explicit interpretation of your experience in the light of key concepts and (especially) hypotheses contained in one or more of the theories treated in the (several sets of) core theoretical readings of the course.

   a. As a rule of thumb, state at least one explicit explanatory, substantive (not methodological), causal hypothesis for every entry. State the hypothesis as an "If . . . , then . . ." statement if possible.

   b. Emphasize core concepts by underlining them for easy review.

   c. Be sure to cite authors' full name, title of article, title of professional journal, magazine, or book; date of publication; and page numbers for each reference cited.

III. *Format and Evaluation*

   A. In the actual writing of the journal, number each page, and date each entry.

   B. Develop an index of the theorists cited in the body and appendices of the journal. For every citation or reference to a theory in the body of the journal, be sure to include a page number of the journal properly referenced in your index. This index will provide a quick check on the thoroughness of your treatment of each theorist or theory of the course. Be sure to treat a majority of the theories somewhere in your journal.

   C. Include an appendix (for each of your two installments) in which you comparatively evaluate the utility of at least three theories used in your journal. The applications compared here should deal with at least one major episode, chapter, case or example (especially as your chosen example concerns change over time (t_1 to t_2), or reaffirmed commitment to some course of action among the members of the group being described).

D. Be sure to evaluate the utility of each theory as you have applied it on each of the four criteria for a good theory, namely:
1. Ease of application
2. Information value
3. Predictive potential, and
4. Explanatory power.
Give a reason and example for your rating on each criterion.

E. This kind of appendix (comparative evaluation of 3 theories) should be part of both installments of your journal (the one done before midterm, and the one done from the midterm to the final class day).

References

Cited in the Text Excluding
Those in Recommended Readings

Bandura, Albert, and R. H. Walters. *Social Learning and Personality Development.* N. Y.: Holt, Rinehart and Winston, 1963.

Biddle, Bruce J., and E. J. Thomas, eds. *Role Theory: Concepts and Research.* N. Y.: Wiley, 1966.

Brim, Orville Jr., and Stanton Wheeler. *Socialization After Childhood.* N. Y.: Wiley, 1966.

Bruyn, Severyn. *The Human Perspective in Sociology: The Methodology of Participant Observation.* Englewood Cliffs, N. J.: Prentice-Hall, 1966.

Buckley, Walter. *Sociology and Modern Systems Theory.* Englewood Cliffs, N. J.: Prentice Hall, 1967.

Carkhuff, R. R., *The Development of Human Resources.* N. Y.: Holt, Rinehart and Winston, 1971.

Cicourel, Aaron. *Cognitive Sociology.* London: Macmillan and Company, 1973.

Clausen, John A., ed. *Socialization and Society.* Boston: Little, Brown, 1968.

Cloward, R. A., and L. E. Ohlin. *Delinquency and Opportunity: A Theory of Delinquent Gangs.* Glencoe, Ill.: Free Press, 1960.

Cohen, A. K., "Research in Delinquent Subcultures." *Journal of Social Issues* 14 (1958), 20–34.

Dollard, John, and N. E. Miller. *Personality and Psychotherapy.* N. Y.: McGraw-Hill, 1950.

Erikson, Erik, ed. *Adulthood.* New York: Norton, 1978.

Gibbons, Don C. *Changing the Lawbreaker.* Englewood Cliffs, N. J.: Prentice-Hall, 1965.

Havighurst, R. J. *Human Development and Education.* N. Y.: Longmans, Green, 1953.

Homans, George C. *The Human Group.* N. Y.: Harcourt, Brace, 1950.
————, *Social Behavior.* N. Y.: D. Harcourt, Brace, Jovanovich, 1961.
James, William. "The Present Dilemma in Philosophy." in *Pragmatism.* Cleveland: World Publishing Co., 1955 ed., 1907.
Kohlberg, L. "The Development of Children's Orientations Toward a Moral Order." 1. Sequence in the development of moral thought, Vita Humana 6 (1963), 11–33.
Lewin, Kurt. *A Dynamic Theory of Personality.* N. Y.: McGraw-Hill, 1935.
Maccoby, Eleanor, "The Development of Moral Values and Behavior in Childhood," pp. 236–237 in J. A. Clausen, ed., *Socialization and Society.* Boston: Little, Brown, 1968.
Muuss, Rolf E. *Theories of Adolescence.* N. Y.: Random House, 1962.
Nisbet, R. A. *Tradition and Revolt.* N. Y.: Random House, 1968.
Piaget, Jean. *The Moral Judgment of the Child.* N. Y.: Harcourt, Brace, 1932.
Rogers, Carl, "This Is Me," pp. 3–27 in *On Becoming a Person.* Boston: Houghton-Mifflin, 1961.
Skinner, B. F. *Verbal Behavior.* N. Y.: Appleton-Century-Crofts, 1957.
Thibaut, J. W., and H. H. Kelley. *The Social Psychology of Groups.* N. Y.: Wiley, 1959.
Walker, Edward, and R. W. Heyns. *An Anatomy for Conformity.* Belmont: Brooks/Cole, 1967.
Warren, Ronald L., "Cultural, Personal and Situational Roles," in *Sociology and Social Research* 34, (1949) 104–111.
Watson, J. B. *Psychology from the Standpoint of a Behaviorist.* Philadelphia: J. B. Lippincott, 1919.

Bibliography

For General Book Recommendations

Aylesworth, Thomas G., and Gerald M. Reagan. *Teaching for Thinking.* Garden City: Doubleday, 1966.

Backman, Carl, and P. Secord, eds. *Problems in Social Psychology.* N. Y.: McGraw-Hill, 1966.

Bennis, Warren, D. E. Berlew, E. Schein, and F. I. Steele, eds. *Interpersonal Dynamics*, 3rd ed. Homewood: Dorsey, 1973.

Bugental, J. F. T., ed. *Challenges of Humanistic Psychology.* N. Y.: McGraw-Hill, 1967.

Coppard, Larry C., and F. L. Goodman, eds. *Urban Gaming/Simulation '77, An Ongoing Conference for Educators and Trainers.* Ann Arbor, Michigan: The University of Michigan, 1977.

Deutsch, Morton, and R. M. Krauss. *Theories in Social Psychology.* N. Y.: Basic Books, 1965.

Fernandez, Ronald, ed. *Social Psychology through Literature.* N. Y.: Wiley, 1972.

Gamson, William, and Andre Modigliani. *Conceptions of Social Life.* Boston: Little, Brown, 1974.

Glass, John F., and J. R. Staude, eds. *Humanistic Society.* Pacific Palisades, California: Goodyear, 1972.

Hollander, Edwin P., and R. G. Hunt, eds. *Current Perspectives in Social Psychology.* N. Y.: Oxford University Press, 1971.

Homans, George C. *The Nature of Social Science.* N. Y.: Harcourt, Brace & World, 1967.

Horn, Robert E., ed., *The Guide to Simulations/Games for Education and Training.* 3rd ed. Cranford, N. J.: Didactic Systems, 1977.

Klietsch, Ronald G. *An Introduction to Learning Games and Instructional Simulations, A Curriculum Guideline.* St. Paul, Minn.: Instructional Simulations & Co., 1969.

Lindesmith, Alfred, A. Strauss, and N. Denzin. *Social Psychology*, 4th ed. Hinsdale, IL: HRW-Dryden, 1975.

Lindzey, Gardner, and E. Aronson, eds. *The Handbook of Social Psychology*, 2nd ed., 5 vol. Reading, Mass.: 1969.

Manis, Jerome G., and Bernard N. Meltzer, eds. *Symbolic Interaction*, 2nd ed. Boston: Allyn & Bacon, 1972.

Marx, Melvin. "The General Nature of Theory Construction," in *Theories in Contemporary Psychology*. N. Y.: McGraw-Hill, 1963.

Maslow, Abraham. *The Psychology of Science*. N. Y.: Harper and Row, 1966.

Pfeiffer, J. William, and John E. Jones, eds. Handbook of Structured Experiences for Human Relations Training, 6 vol. La Jolla: University Associates Press, 1969–1977.

Polanyi, Michael. *Personal Knowledge*. Chicago: University of Chicago Press, 1962.

Progoff, Ira. *At a Journal Workshop*. N. Y.: Dialogue House Library, 1975.

Rogers, Carl R. *Freedom to Learn*. Columbus, Ohio: Charles E. Merrill Publishing Co., 1969.

Sahakian, William S., ed. *Social Psychology*. Scranton: Intext Educational Publishers, 1972.

Schellenberg, James A. *Masters of Social Psychology*. N. Y.: Oxford University Press, 1978.

Shank, Theodore J. *A Digest of 500 Plays*. London: Collier Books, 1963.

Shaw, Marvin E., and Philip R. Costanzo. *Theories of Social Psychology*. N. Y.: McGraw-Hill, 1970.

Slawski, Carl, "Evaluating Theories Comparatively," Zeitschrift für Soziologie 3, 4 (October 1974): 397–408.

Stadsklev, Ron. *Handbook of Simulation Gaming in Social Education*. (Part 1: Textbook; Part 2: Directory, 2nd ed.). The University of Alabama, 1974 & 1980.

Steffensen, James Jr., ed. *Great Scenes from the World Theater*, 2 vol. N. Y.: Avon, 1965

Zetterberg, Hans. *On Theory and Verification in Sociology*. Totowa, N. J.: Bedminster Press, 1963.

Alternate
Table of Contents

The general topics of the selected readings, introduced earlier in Appendix B, are here partially cross-classified by chapter number and author. Many articles appear in several categories.The topics given here correspond more closely to the traditional ones treated in courses in social psychology.

The instructor could easily develop his own table of contents with this chart as a guide. The recommended readings are all readily available, nearly all reprinted, and could be put on a reserve bookshelf in the library.

General Topic	Laboratory	Participant Observation Or Case Study	Survey: Questionnaire Or Interview	Mostly Theory
Self or Personality		1(Wheelis)		1(Maslow), 13 (Meltzer), 16(Schutz)
Communication				8(Rapoport), 13(Meltzer), 3(Cartwright & Schein), 5(Milgram), 1(Maslow)
Attitude Change	9(Cohen & Brehm), 6(Bandura & Skinner)	7(Homans & McCall)	11(Backman et al.)	14(Scheff), 8(Rapoport), 4(Goode), 12(Lecky), 13(Meltzer), 1(Maslow), 3(Cartwright & Schein), 5(Deutsch & Milgram), 2(Elkind)
Motivation	6(Bandura & Skinner)			4(Goode), 7(Homans & McCall), 2(Elkind), 3(Cartwright & Schein), 1(Maslow & Wheelis)
Social Perception		7(Homans & McCall)	10(Newcomb, Levinger & Breedlove), 11(Backman et al.)	14(Scheff), 7(Homans & McCall), 8(Rapoport), 6(Bandura & Skinner), 15(Goffman), 16(Schutz), 1(Maslow & Wheelis)
Close Relationships, Friendships			10(Newcomb, Levinger & Breedlove)	2(Elkind), 15(Goffman), 1(Maslow
Roles	6(Bandura & Skinner)			4(Goode), 7(Homans & McCall), 13(Meltzer), 2(Elkind)
Deviance				14(Scheff), 4(Goode), 3(Cartwright)
Conflict	3(Cartwright)		11(Backman et al.)	14(Scheff), 4(Goode), 8(Rapoport), 5(Deutsch) 16(Schutz), 15(Goffman)
Ecology (Space & Time)				5(Milgram)
Organizations				5(Milgram)
Cross-Cultural				16(Schutz)
Inter-Group Relations				13(Shibutani)*

*This chapter was recommended, not selected nor introduced above.

Index

Angel Street, analysis of, 55–57, 96–99, 122–26

Backman, C. W., 83, 161
Bandura, A., 63, 154
Becker, H., 105
Behavioristic theories, 60–68, critique of, 69–76
Biddle, B. J., 52
Breedlove, J., 160
Brehm, J. W., 159
Brim, O., Jr., 23
Bruyn, S., 130
Buckley, W., 133

Carkhuff, R. R., 73
Cartwright, D., 40, 147
Cicourel, A., 111
Cloward, R. A., 52
Cognitive dissonance, 77, 79–80, 88; analysis of, 4, 89–90, 97–98, 129, 131, 134, 138, 172; application of, 99
Cohen, A. K., 52, 159
Conflict, 46, 49–50, 70, 172
Congruency theories, 60–61, 77–87, 101; critique of, 88–99
Cooley, C. H., 21

Deutsch, M., 49, 70, 80, 152, 157
Dissonance, 79, 80
Dollard, J., 63
Dramaturgy, 100–101, 109–10;

analysis of, 120–22, 130, 132, 136, 138, 172

Ease of application, 11, 12
Elkind, D., 145
Ellsberg, D., 120
Erikson, E., 23–24, 26, 28, 29, 61, 101, 145, 147
Ethnomethodology, 100, 111–13, 115; analysis of, 122, 129, 132, 136, 138, 172
Exchange theory, 65–66; analysis of, 130, 132, 133, 136, 137, 172; application of, 60, 65–66, 73–74, 122–25
Explanatory power, 12–13, 14

Festinger, L., 79
Freud, S., 145

Game theory, 66–68, 69; analysis of, 130, 132, 136, 138, 172; application of, 60, 74–75
Gandhi, M., 25, 118
Garfinkel, H., 111, 112, 113
General systems theory, 9, 127, 133–34, 172
Gibbons, D. C., 29
Goffman, E., 109, 112, 168
Goode, W. J., 40, 44, 150, 151
Group dynamics, 41–43, 69; analysis of, 129, 132, 135–36, 137; application of, 50–51, 55–59

Hamilton, P., 55
Havighurst, R. J., 23
Heynes, R. W., 71
Hobbes, T., 9
Homans, G. C., 2, 65
Hull, C., 62, 71
Humanistic-development theories,
    18–25, 40, 70; critique of, 26–38
Hypothesis, 2–3

Identity development, 23–25, 61;
    analysis of, 132, 137; application
    of, 28–30
Information value, 12, 13–14
Interparty conflict, 46–48; analysis
    of, 128, 132, 135, 137; application
    of, 54–55
Interpersonal congruence, 77, 83–
    84, analysis of, 129, 132, 135,
    138, 172; application of 92–94

James, W., 15
Jones, J. E., 171

Kelley, H. H., 65
Kohlberg, L., 23
Krauss, R. M., 80
Kwan, K. M., 124

Labeling theory, 100, 105–8, 115;
    analysis of, 130, 132, 136, 138,
    172; application of, 118–20
Lecky, P., 77, 86, 163
Lemert, E., 105, 106
Levinger, G., 160
Lewin, K., 69

Maccoby, E., 23
Marx, K., 70
Marx, M., 5, 7
Maslow, A., 15, 20, 26, 55, 56, 143,
    144
McCall, M., 156
Mead, G. H., 100, 101, 164, 165
Meltzer, B., 164
Milgram, S., 21, 49, 70, 152
Miller, N. E., 63

Nader, R., 120
Newcomb, T., 81, 160
Nisbet, R. A., 15
Nixon, R., 85

Ohlin, L. E., 52

Pfeiffer, W., 171
Piaget, J., 23
Pierce, J., 161
Predictability, 12, 14

Rapoport, A., 157
Rogers, C., 15
Role bargaining, 43–45, 70, 88;
    analysis of, 97, 98, 130, 132, 133,
    136, 137, 172; application of,
    51–54, 96–98

Scheff, T., 105, 166
Schein, E. H., 40, 148
Schultz, A., 169
Schweitzer, A., 118
Secord, P. F., 83, 161
Self-consistency theory, 77, 86–87,
    88; analysis of, 129, 132, 135,
    138, 172; application of, 95–96
Shakespeare, W., 3
Shibutani, T., 124
Shirts, R. G., 150, 171
Simmel, G., 46, 55, 70, 152
Simulation games, 59, 171–74
Skinner, B. F., 64, 71
Slawski, C., 11
Social actualization theory, 20–22;
    analysis of, 172; application of, 4,
    27–28, 55, 56–59
Social interaction theories, 61,
    100–14; critique of, 115–26
Social scientists, task roles of, 130–
    33
Solzhenitsyn, A., 122
Stimulus-response behaviorism,
    60, 62–64, 101, analysis of, 129,
    133, 135, 137, 172; application of,
    64, 70–72
Structure and change theories, 39–
    48, 101; critique of, 49–59

Sullivan, H. S., 101
Symbolic interactionism, 61, 88, 101–5, 109, 115; analysis of, 124, 125, 126–130, 132, 133, 136–37, 138, 172; application of, 117–18, 123–25
Symmetry, 77, 81–82, 88; analysis of, 129, 131, 134–35, 138, 172; application of, 90–91

Theory, definition of, 1–2, 3, 130–31; evaluation of, 1–17

Theory construction, modes of, 5–8
Thibaut, J. W., 65
Thomas, E. J., 52

Walker, E., 71
Walters, R. H., 63
Warren, R. L., 43
Watson, J. B., 62
Wheelis, A. B., 143
Wheeler, S., 23

Zetterberg, H., 2